What Others Say

"your home — a lighthouse is the most thorough, understandable, creative, detailed guide of an inductive Bible study I have ever seen . . . it can't help but touch many."

ann kiemel anderson
author, lecturer

"An eminently practical book like this does not come along too often, and the witness of this book on using a home environment for effective witness is most refreshing. The informality, modeling and setting for home evangelism provides a unique opportunity for many who might be uncomfortable in other situations. These guidelines are helpful, practical and eminently workable. This will prove to be a challenge to all — particularly Christian couples who enjoy their home. The 'success' testimonies are most encouraging."

Ted W. Engstrom
President
World Vision

"God's plan is to use the Christian home as a base for evangelism . . . In *Your Home, a Lighthouse,* Bob and Betty Jacks have combined inspiring example with practical teaching about this method."

Robert A. Cook
Chancellor
The King's College

YOUR HOME A LIGHTHOUSE

BOB & BETTY JACKS
with Ron Wormser, Sr.

A resource from

Churches Alive!
MINISTERING TO THE CHURCHES OF THE WORLD
Box 3800, San Bernardino, California 92413

Published by
NAVPRESS ⬤°
A MINISTRY OF THE NAVIGATORS
P.O. Box 6000, Colorado Springs, Colorado 80934

© 1986, Churches Alive International
Revised edition © 1987
All rights reserved, including translation
Library of Congress No. 87-060179
ISBN: 0-89109-127-0
11270

Cover illustration by Per Volquartz

Printed in the United States of America

CONTENTS

Because we share kindred aims for helping local churches fulfill Christ's Great Commission to "go and make disciples," NavPress and Churches Alive have joined efforts on certain strategic publishing projects that are intended to bring effective disciplemaking resources into the service of the local church.

For more than a decade, Churches Alive has teamed up with churches of all denominations to establish vigorous disciplemaking ministries. At the same time, NavPress has focused on publishing Bible studies, books, and other resources that have grown out of The Navigators' 50 years of disciplemaking experience.

Now, together, we're working to offer special products like this one that are designed to stimulate a deeper, more fruitful commitment to Christ in the local gatherings of His Church.

In appreciation . . .

. . . for Mike, Beth and Matt, who, through their growing years, made it easy for us to reach out to others by their positive spirit, cheerful babysitting and prayer concern.

. . . and for the continuing joy they give us as they also tell others of God's love.

About the Authors

Bob and Betty Jacks grew up in Parkersburg, West Virginia, met as teenagers in a small church there and married when Bob was a Junior in college.

After completing college, Bob worked in engineering research with the DuPont Company for twenty years before going on with his cousin to establish their own business.

Bob and Betty have three children, Michael, Beth and Matthew. Making their home in Connecticut, they are dedicated to the ministry of their local church.

A primary focus of their lives over the past twenty years has been to extend the ministry of their church into the surrounding area through home Bible studies. Without formal Christian education, but drawing upon their vast experience in the business community, they have learned to communicate the gospel to non-Christians in informal settings with astounding effectiveness.

Significantly, what they have learned and used so fruitfully has been reproduced in the lives of others. Through the pages of this book, these proven methods for effective informal evangelism are now available to you and all who want to better serve our Lord by reaching still others.

Ron Wormser Sr. is a writer and Director of Media for Churches Alive International, with 35 years of experience in ministry to local churches.

Foreword

Life begets life!

Bob and Betty Jacks clearly illustrate this principle. For twenty years, they have allowed the life of our Lord to work in and through them to reproduce new life in others.

They have developed a simple concept for using the warmth of a home as a setting in which people are more relaxed and given to considering God, His Word and the implications for their lives.

The result has been a continuing personal growth and unusual effectiveness in channeling new believers into churches where they mature and become equipped for ministry.

I've known Bob and Betty for many years and have grown to love them and respect their faithfulness and effectiveness.

Out of gratitude to Christ, they are helping to make this outstanding, proven guide to evangelistic home Bible studies available to you through the ministry of Churches Alive International.

Their reward? — Your joy and fruitfulness to the glory of our Lord!

Howard Ball, 1986
President
Churches Alive International

Things I can guarantee

"There are a couple of *things I can guarantee in life*," says Bob Jacks, as he speaks to a group of some 30 men and women who gathered to learn how to use their homes to reach others for Christ.

"One is that if you believe in Jesus Christ as your Savior, you're going to heaven.

"Number two is that if you follow these guidelines for an evangelistic home Bible study, you will have success."

As he speaks, you find your heart responding. You begin to believe that reaching others for Christ in your home is possible, and could even be enjoyable.

Bob is quiet in his mannerisms. His unassuming ways seem out of proportion to his large and aggressive faith. What he and his wife Betty have been doing so effectively for some 20 years, anyone can do — in neighborhoods, on the job, on campuses or in overseas missionary work.

As you measure his words, you see the foundations for his deep-seated convictions: the power of the Word of God, prayer and the Holy Spirit, resources available to every Christian.

Our prayer is that these pages will renew your mind to the excitement of God's enabling power for ministry. And may the simple procedures outlined here give liberating freedom to you, either as leader or host, to begin a home Bible study through which many will come to Christ.

You can, you know.

Part One —
Our Beginning

My one compelling purpose

Larry

If there was anything I didn't need, it was to add "just another meeting" to my already overcrowded schedule. So why get involved in helping to start a home Bible study?

My one compelling purpose was to reach out to people who were unlikely to ever attend a church where the message of Jesus Christ is clearly presented. And I am convinced that such people are probably in the majority in most communities.

With this motivation was the conviction that it would be hard to find a more conducive atmosphere to help people enter a personal relationship with Christ than the warmth and informality of a home.

Where better to relate to both husbands and wives simultaneously . . . to develop loving, concerned relationships . . . and to share the relevance of the Bible as an "operating manual" for life and not just a handbook for emergencies.

Using laymen to lead and avoiding denominational emphases, we found that we could develop a non-threatening atmosphere where people would voice their problems. God honored the simple sharing of His Word and lives were changed.

While I am totally committed to my local church, I thank God for helping me see that a lifetime could be spent in church "activities" with no real productivity. I want to use my time and talents efficiently for the Lord. For me, this means investing a portion of my life in my community where needy people live.

Chapter 1

The Bible Study Nobody Wanted

Bob and Betty Jacks

Nobody, but nobody, wanted to help begin a Bible study for non-Christians.

At the mention of reaching out to non-Christians, almost any audience experiences a parade of fears. The fear of the unknown . . . the fear of inviting . . . the fear of rejection . . . the fear of what to teach . . . the fear of questions . . . the fear of how to present the gospel . . . the fear of a "no"-response.

So, in retrospect, the fact that no one wanted to help start an evangelistic home Bible study was not unusual. But it did seem incongruous to the climate of the church we were attending.

For the first eight years of our married life, we had attended four different churches. Now we were in a church that was different. We were learning what it means to have a personal relationship with Jesus Christ.

This was a large church with a strong emphasis on missions. They had a large budget and helped to support over 50 missionaries. The pastoral staff, deacons and Sunday School teachers talked about the importance of sharing our faith. But after hearing this for two or three years, we began to look around and realized that our church's total effort seemed directed toward people half a world away. Little action was being taken for the world at our doorstep.

We displayed the banners of Vacation Bible School, Boys' Clubs, Girls' Clubs and evangelistic meetings. We prayed for new people to come to our church and for people to commit their lives to Jesus Christ. Virtually no one, however, seemed to risk venturing out into the deep water to cast their nets among neighbors and work associates who, typically, would never come to a church.

Most of us find it easier to fish for men and women as long as we can stand on the dock. We feel a security within the walls of our church buildings, but that's not where the fish are.

We have a place on the ocean in Maine. Our sons fish off the dock, and we know exactly what they are going to catch — very small mackerel. It's "so-so" fishing, not all that exciting. But once in a while, we will rent a deep sea charter boat with an old salt named Bill. That takes a commitment of time and money. We spend two hours getting to the fishing site and never know what we are going to catch. But one thing is sure, it's much more exciting than fishing off the dock. The catch can be large cod, halibut, haddock and even shark.

I believe this is one way we need to apply Jesus' teaching:

> One day as he was preaching on the shore of Lake Gennesaret, great crowds pressed in on him to listen to the Word of God. He noticed two empty boats standing at the water's edge while the fishermen washed their nets.

Stepping into one of the boats, Jesus asked Simon, its owner, to push out a little into the water, so that he could sit in the boat and speak to the crowds from there.

When he had finished speaking, he said to Simon, "Now go out where it is deeper and let down your nets and you will catch a lot of fish!"

"Sir," Simon replied, "we worked hard all last night and didn't catch a thing. But if you say so, we'll try again."

And this time their nets were so full that they began to tear! A shout for help brought their partners in the other boat and soon both boats were filled with fish and on the verge of sinking.

When Simon Peter realized what had happened, he fell to his knees before Jesus and said, "Oh, sir, please leave us — I'm too much of a sinner for you to have around." For he was awestruck by the size of their catch, as were the others with him, and his partners too — James and John, the sons of Zebedee. Jesus replied, *"Don't be afraid! From now on you'll be fishing for the souls of men!"*

And as soon as they landed, they left everything and went with him (Luke 5:1-11, emphasis added).

Let's not be content with only fishing off the dock of our church buildings; let's not neglect the deep. The disciples had a great catch, recognizing that it was purely the Lord's doing.

We can expect God to honor our obedience and fill our nets if we launch out into the deep to "catch men." That "deep" can be your neighborhood, office or campus, wherever your world is.

What about Jerusalem? . . .

There's a tendency to work for a great missionary effort in Judea, Samaria and the uttermost parts of the world and miss our Jerusalem, our own neighborhood. A church may have large numerical growth, but is evangelism taking place? Or, is the growth from Christians moving into the community or drawing people from other churches?

Along with all the good already happening in and through our churches, we need to open our lives to those outside. We need to tap the reservoirs of our churches so the living water may flow out to meet the needs of others and help bring them to Christ.

Back in 1965, God was growing that kind of desire in our hearts. We knew the chairman of the church Board and the chairmen of the Missionary Committee and Christian Education Committee. We knew all the leaders. We invited them and others. Soon, sixteen couples began to study and discuss the Bible together.

A vision shared . . .

After about six months into the Bible study, we decided, "This is good news. Why don't we suggest to the group that we break up into eight groups of two couples each and share this good news with our neighbors and folks at work?" We went to the next Saturday night study with great enthusiasm. We told them our plan. . . Zero response. And we went home feeling like whipped pups.

Three months later, one of the couples, Sandy and Larry, came to us and said, "We've been thinking about what you suggested, and we'd like to try to start one of these evangelistic home Bible studies." You would think the four of us would have been off and running immediately. But, no, we kept saying, "We'll start" . . . "We'll start" . . . "We'll start."

Nothing happened until we met together and nailed down a date. "O.K., we're going to start the first Friday in October." Now we were committed. We picked a leader, someone who would be sensitive to non-Christians and had the knowledge to lead a study. We invited people, agreeing not to ask any

Christians. The study began with about 25 of our friends and acquaintances.

The missing ingredient . . .

Everything was going great for four or five months when we suddenly realized that even though all of the other people in the study were non-Christians (as far as we knew), no one was coming to Christ. At that time, we made what was probably the most important decision we could have made about this outreach to non-Christians. We decided that we needed to pray.

We met together with the other couple who hosted the study. We were joined by a doctor friend and his wife who wanted to start another study. Together, we prayed. We prayed, by name, for the people who were coming to the study. We prayed specifically for their needs and that they would yield their lives to Christ. All of a sudden, people started making decisions for Christ.

We met with those two couples one Saturday night a month for ten years, praying for the spiritually needy in "our world." To add a little dimension to that Saturday night, we called it a prayer supper. The host couple would prepare the main course and the others would bring everything else. It was one of the highlights of our ministry, exciting and fun.

From that time on, prayer became an essential part of our Bible study plan. Our Bible study meets monthly, but every leader or host couple meets twice a month, once for the study and once for prayer.

Out of that original study, over a ten-year period, some 25 groups were born. There were study groups at work, in people's neighborhoods, in schools, and couples', women's and men's studies. The outreach grew to where, at one time, there were about 400 people a month who were hearing the claims of Christ who otherwise may never have been touched with the gospel.

Even in New England . . .

When we moved from Delaware to Connecticut, people said, "Don't expect this to work here. You're in New England now. People are cold and hard. They're just not going to respond." But we did expect it to work, we did start the studies and people did respond. And the approach is working today.

As you look at the lostness of the world in which you live, I'm sure you will agree that, as Christians, we must do something to help reach these people for Christ. The task is not hopeless. There is something you can do. If God has placed an urgency in your heart to share His love with others, prayerfully consider how He wants you to be involved. Perhaps it can be as a part of a home Bible study.

We will be sharing in detail what we do and what we have learned over 20 years of outreach through evangelistic home Bible studies. Even though most of the emphasis will be on a couples' study approach, the principles and methods also apply to study groups for men, women, singles, the campus, missions, church planting and more.

We know in advance what your response will be. "It's so simple."

That's true. It's simple, but God has honored this simplicity and dependence upon Him and His Word. *We have never seen a study fail that has followed these guidelines.*

And either as a leader or as a host of a couples' or women's or men's study, there is a place for you to participate.

For further study —
Matthew 4:18-5:16

Scores of people came to Christ

Arlene

I grew up in a very "religious" home and had always been faithful in attending church. Even though I considered myself "religious," I had a great fear of dying. At my grandmother's funeral, I kept wondering where she was. I really didn't have an answer.

When my best friend, Barbara, invited me to a women's home Bible study, I saw no need for it in my life. But as a result of her persistence, I finally attended a Bible study at her home. Mind you, I did this against my will and to do her a favor.

The thing that amazed me was the friendliness of the women and the fact that no one discussed religion or church. But even with the friendly atmosphere, I didn't really look forward to going to the group. I was afraid they were trying to change my religion.

My girl friend moved away, and one of the women who sponsored the study became a customer at the beauty salon I ran. Through her sharing and loving concern, I later made a personal commitment to Christ.

Soon after my decision, my husband Bob and our two children made the same commitment. A short time later, we started a women's study and a couples' study in our home. Over a period of eight years, *scores of people came to Christ,* including my parents and several members of my immediate family.

My daughter, who was a high school student at the time, started a Bible study in our home with the help of a well-known youth ministry. Several High Schoolers came to Christ through that effort. One of those who accepted Christ is now her husband.

Bob and I started a couples' study when we moved to another state. Over a three-year period, we saw approximately 25 people accept Christ.

We came to Christ approximately ten years ago and have sponsored Bible studies in our home on a continuous basis. We have seen the tremendous effectiveness, through this ministry, in bringing people to Christ and helping them become faithful disciples.

Chapter 2

The Tip of an Iceberg

Betty Jacks

We don't do it often enough, but if we stop and look back, we can see God's hand at work in our lives. His guidance, blessings and the fruit He has harvested in and through our lives are great cause for praise.

Seldom, however, do Christians look ahead with an eye of faith to appreciate what great harvests can result from small beginnings. We are geared to instant gratification. Our tendency is to exalt large numbers and quick responses.

Even now, as you envision a Bible study in your home, you may be thinking of a group of 15 or 20 or more. If that happens, praise God. But I rejoice in a study beginning with even three or four. Again and again, I have seen how just one person reached through a Bible study is the tip of an iceberg through whom an abundant reaping results.

For the first five or six years of our study group ministry, I was a babysitter. I felt babysitting was important to allow young mothers who were coming to feel comfortable about their children's needs being met. The first person young mothers see when they come to a study is the babysitter.

Then God opened a ministry to the "tip of an iceberg."

God opens doors . . .

Barbara, my hairdresser, had a beauty salon in the basement of her home and did the hair of many of the women in the neighborhood. One Friday, I went to get my hair done. Barbara asked where I was going that evening. When I said, "To a Bible study," she couldn't believe it. To a Bible study on Friday night! She couldn't see much fun in that. But this opened the door to talking about Christ on future visits.

Soon Barbara invited Christ into her life. An enthusiastic new believer, she said, "You spoke about a Bible study. Could you help me start a Bible study for women in my neighborhood?"

We began the study together. One woman who came was Arlene, who was also a hairdresser. When Barbara and her husband moved away, Arlene began doing my hair, giving me more opportunity to talk with her about Christ.

When Arlene told me about her eight-year-old son being unable to sleep at night because of nightmares, I gave her a little booklet that tells how to become a Christian. Excited about the booklet, Arlene wanted to share this good news with her son.

One night when he awoke from a nightmare, she read the booklet to him to calm him down. It included a prayer at the end, which he repeated after her. Several weeks later, when Arlene told me that her son had stopped having nightmares, I told her that he must have received Christ! Arlene said, "What do you mean?"

Apparently, her son had understood the booklet with a simple childlike faith, while the message had escaped her. I explained what it meant to be a Christian and Arlene, too, received Christ.

The circle widens . . .

Arlene wanted to reach her husband. I suggested, "Why don't you start a couples' Bible study? He'll have to come if it's in your house."

"What would I have to do?" Arlene asked.

"Well, can you make phone calls and coffee?"

"Oh, yes, I can do that," she replied.

"Fine, Bob and I will do the rest," I assured her.

Several women from the neighborhood came, but Arlene and her husband, Bob, were the only couple who attended. After about six months, he received Christ.

Later, we had a Christmas potluck and they invited all their neighbors. With that new impetus, the study grew to about 40 people, lasted eight years and many people became Christians through it. Arlene was not content with just the couples' study. She also started a women's study and it was equally effective.

When Bob and I moved to Connecticut, Bob and Arlene moved with us. Bob was one of the managers of a new business my husband and his cousin began there. About six months after we moved, we started another Bible study, with Bob and Arlene serving as a host couple. Another 20 or 25 people came to Christ through that group.

It's incredible what God will do with small beginnings when we are faithful in doing our part.

All that I have told about Bob and Arlene is just a larger "tip of the iceberg."

There's more . . .

Shortly after Arlene became a Christian, she developed a concern for her family who were of another faith. She drove two hours to her mother's home to tell her what had happened in her life, totally unprepared for her mother's response: "I can't believe that you are turning your back on the way I have raised you." Crushed, Arlene cried all the way home.

She called to tell me what had happened. "Well, why don't we just really pray about that?" I said. "You know, maybe you should start a Bible study at your sister's home up there. Do you think she would do that?"

Arlene said, "That's two hours away."

"Bob and I will go up once a month to lead the study, if your sister will hostess it," I told her.

Arlene's sister reluctantly agreed, and after about six months she received Christ. Then, in sequence, her husband, four children and mother became Christians. Finally, Alice, Arlene's sister, led her father to Christ.

While all of this was happening, Bob's and Arlene's oldest daughter became a Christian, and I get goosebumps as I think about how she has reproduced spiritually both in high school and college.

Bob and Arlene moved again, and the same story was repeated. Obviously, not everyone reached through a home Bible study becomes the catalyst that Bob and Arlene have been in reaching so many others. Arlene had been a Christian for only two months when she started her first study. And Bob began inviting men from his work when he had

Barbara's Bible Study

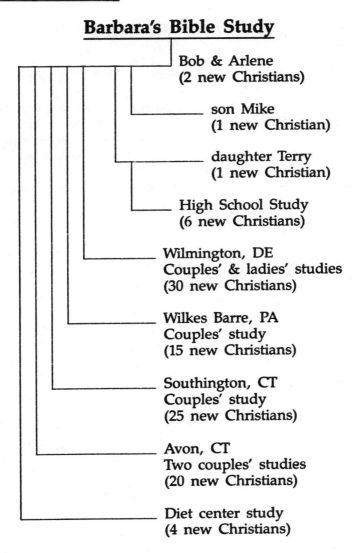

Bob & Arlene
(2 new Christians)

son Mike
(1 new Christian)

daughter Terry
(1 new Christian)

High School Study
(6 new Christians)

Wilmington, DE
Couples' & ladies' studies
(30 new Christians)

Wilkes Barre, PA
Couples' study
(15 new Christians)

Southington, CT
Couples' study
(25 new Christians)

Avon, CT
Two couples' studies
(20 new Christians)

Diet center study
(4 new Christians)

A total of 104 new Christians
from 1 Bible study

been a Christian for only a month. But, this is not intended as an example to emulate or a measure of success.

On the contrary. We only want to encourage you not to place an unnecessary burden upon yourself in feeling that you cannot launch a ministry unless it will be a spectacular ministry from the very start. It was not spectacular to sit in a Bible study with only Bob and me and Bob and Arlene and a couple of women, but was it worthwhile!

Would we do it over again? You be the judge of that.

For further study —
John 1:35-51

The first time I had ever heard

Nancy

My father left our family when I was two, and my mother died when I was nine, leaving me to be raised by my sister. I went to church as a young person and did all of the things I was supposed to do, but never felt fulfilled. As soon as I was old enough to make my own decision, I stopped attending.

I was married, and a few years later my husband and I had a child. I felt fulfilled for a time, but several years later my world collapsed. My husband, a police officer, was shot and killed. I realized then that I really had no control over my life. My little world that used to be so comfortable and neat was no longer.

I tried to escape, moving to another state and buying all the things I thought would bring happiness. Loneliness and futility brought me back to my former environment, where I settled in with a new home and a mortgage.

Then I met Kevin, to whom I am now married. We lived the paradox of being very much in love, but also very lonely people. My child and his two by a previous marriage didn't fill the void. We were grasping at anything when a friend encouraged me to attend a home Bible study.

I resisted at first, but later went. It was *the first time I had ever heard* the Bible presented so plainly and simply. I understood how I could receive Christ into my life. I didn't all of a sudden say, "That's what I want; I can do it right now." But after several studies, the assurance settled in that Jesus wanted me to be His child and I responded. It was as though a load was lifted from my shoulders. I knew this was what I had been searching for. Later, Kevin attended a study and also received Christ.

I'm still growing and learning, and I know that I still have a long way to go. But when I think of the way my life was before and what it is like now . . . well, there is just no way you could begin to compare the difference. And I know it's because of the home study.

Chapter 3

Thoughts for Winning

Bob Jacks

When you launch an evangelistic home Bible study, you cross enemy lines. You have a specific purpose, to communicate the love of Jesus Christ in a way that others will be drawn to Him as Savior and Lord. Of course, as soon as people become Christians, you add a second dimension to your study, to help them grow and communicate the love of God to others.

In this spiritual battle, Satan will not give up his territory easily. Your preparation must include an understanding of the nature of the task and the provision God has made for you. For this reason, I want to give you some of the Scriptures that have been meaningful to me as I have led these studies.

I pray you will not just read, but meditate upon each one of these important truths.

Your task . . .

So everywhere we go we talk about Christ to all who will listen, warning them and teaching them as well as

we know how. We want to be able to present each one
to God, perfect because of what Christ has done for each
of them. This is my work, and I can do it only because
Christ's mighty energy is at work within me (Colossians
1:28,29).

The purpose of the home study group is to
present Jesus Christ. You don't talk about denominations, controversial issues or your church. You don't
use lofty words or brilliant ideas. You talk about
Jesus.

And how do you do this? Just as well as you
know how. You don't have to possess all knowledge
or have all the skills in the world. No one is that
gifted by God. All you can do is your best with the
gifts God has given you. Yet, along with God's
delegation of the task is Christ's mighty energy
available to work within you!

God's power is greater than your fear . . .

Dear Brothers, even when I first came to you I didn't
use lofty words and brilliant ideas to tell you God's message. For I decided that I would speak only of Jesus Christ
and his death on the cross. I came to you in weakness —
timid and trembling. And my preaching was very plain,
not with a lot of oratory and human wisdom, but the
Holy Spirit's power was in my words, proving to those
who heard them that the message was from God. I did
this because I wanted your faith to stand firmly upon
God, not on man's great ideas. Yet when I am among
mature Christians I do speak with words of great wisdom,
but not the kind that comes from here on earth, and not
the kind that appeals to the great men of this world, who
are doomed to fall (1 Corinthians 2:1-6).

Paul, that giant of the faith, was fearful! Little
wonder, then, that I, and everybody I have worked
with in Bible studies, have been gripped with fear

in launching a new group. But the new groups were started because of a willingness to walk by faith, regardless of the fear. It takes someone with a burden for people that's bigger than his fear.

You don't go by feelings. In faith you communicate Jesus Christ and Him crucified, and your ministry, like Paul's, can be a demonstration of the "Holy Spirit's power."

Allow the Holy Spirit to do His work through you . . .

Then Peter preached a long sermon, telling about Jesus and strongly urging all his listeners to save themselves from the evils of their nation. And those who believed Peter were baptized — about 3,000 in all! (Acts 2:40,41).

This tremendous response came as the result of Peter's famous message at Pentecost. The Holy Spirit, of Whom Peter spoke, filled and controlled his life. Peter's boldness and fruitfulness utterly contradicted his earlier denial of Christ. Again, it was the Holy Spirit working in him.

That same Holy Spirit desires to empower you for service for Christ. Just as you have received Jesus Christ by faith to be your Savior and Lord, so, by faith, you can allow the Holy Spirit to fill and control your life. You do not have to minister in your own strength alone. The resources of God are yours through His indwelling Spirit.

Don't Play "Holy Spirit" . . .

But the fact of the matter is that it is best for you that I go away, for if I don't, the Comforter won't come. If I do, he will — for I will send him to you. And when he has come he will convince the world of its sin, and of the availability of God's goodness, and of deliverance from

judgment. The world's sin is unbelief in me; there is
righteousness available because I go to the Father and
you shall see me no more; there is deliverance from
judgment because the prince of this world has already
been judged (John 16:7-11).

What freedom in knowing it is not our responsibility to convince other people of their sin and
need of Christ. If we take upon ourselves the work
God intended for the Holy Spirit to do, we cause
pressures in our relationships that hinder others
from coming to Christ. Allowing the Holy Spirit to
do His work liberates us to be ourselves and
strengthens our rapport with the non-Christian.

Relax, others want to hear . . .

For when we brought you the Good News, it was not
just meaningless chatter to you; no, you listened with
great interest. What we told you produced a powerful
effect upon you, for the Holy Spirit gave you great and
full assurance that what we said was true. And you know
how our very lives were further proof to you of the truth
of our message. So you became our followers and the
Lord's; for you received our message with joy from the
Holy Spirit in spite of the trials and sorrows it brought
you (1 Thessalonians 1:5,6).

I think the average Christian thinks the world
really doesn't want to hear about Christ. We just
know this person doesn't want to hear and that
person is not interested. But what does this verse
say? "You received our message with joy from the
Holy Spirit in spite of the trials and sorrows it
brought you." Your own life and the lives of the
millions of Christians in the world today all testify
that others do want to hear about Jesus.

Enjoy being with them . . .

For the Holy Spirit, God's gift, does not want you to be afraid of people, but to be wise and strong, and to love them and enjoy being with them (2 Timothy 1:7).

Fear may come, and it does, but you don't have to let it stay. God wants to remove the fear and give you joy in being with non-Christians. Leading or hosting an evangelistic home Bible study is not a penalty, it is a privilege. The people in your Bible study are not a threat to your joy. Allow the Holy Spirit to make them a source of joy as you see God change lives. Some of the most exciting Christians in my world today were non-Christians who came to a study and are now not only Christians but vital reproducers. Being used by God to reach others puts a vitality in their lives that makes them a joy to know.

Take your resources and go . . .

It is really not the job of our pastors to bring people to Christ. Their job is to help us worship God and to help enhance our relationship with Him. It is the responsibility of sheep to reproduce.

I am told it takes 22 laymen working one year for every person who comes to Christ. If we were used-car salesmen, with that record our company would go bankrupt. Yet, Betty and I are working with a couple who started with a Bible study six months after their commitment to Christ. In only seven months they had reproduced 14 new Christians. Filled with the Holy Spirit, you, too, can be fruitful in ministry, but there is a cost.

First, this ministry requires committed people, people who have a burden for those outside of Christ. Ideally, you need two host couples and a leader couple (if it's a men's or women's study, two hosts and a leader). Single adults should have a team of three to five people.

Second, this ministry calls you and your team to obedience, to be individuals ready to break out of the walls of the church, away from being a spectator into the action arena. And, if you follow the guidelines set in this book, you are going to have a successful study.

Third, this ministry will bring you and your team face to face with people whose ways of life and philosophies are alien to the gospel — people who are looking, but who are sometimes obstinately opposed to Christianity as they know it. Pray for understanding about why they think the way they do. Often, those who are most obstinate become most fruitful. Your secret for success in reaching them is love, the love of Christ constraining you and overflowing your life to envelop them.

**For further study —
Colossians 1:9-19**

Part Two —
Your Beginning

God had been preparing me

Dave

My motivation to get involved in hosting and later leading a home Bible study grew over a period of time.

A friend died of cancer and woke me to the fact that people are dying every day without Christ . . . I passed a derelict on the street and heard a voice inside me saying, "You know, I love him no less than I love you." . . . Driving through my neighborhood observing people playing, mowing lawns, and pulling weeds, I thought again of the words, "You know, I love them no less than I love you." . . . Someone who has meant a lot to me in my personal growth told me that when he drives through his neighborhood he prays for the names he sees on the mailboxes. I began to pray specifically for my neighbors.

I was aware that something was happening in my life. When I was approached to have a Bible study in my home, I recognized that *God had been preparing me,* so I agreed that I would and set a date for the first study.

God's preparation didn't relieve all my fears. It's one thing to share Christ with someone away from your home; you can always leave that situation. But when you're in the neighborhood, you continue living with those people. We had some insecurity about how people would react.

We found that people are much more receptive to hearing about Christ in a comfortable home setting. That washed away our fears.

I have grown by leaps and bounds by being involved. My prayer life has been greatly enhanced. Some of my selfishness is gone, and my prayers have become more focused on other people.

Frankly, I don't know of any other ministry that offers a greater potential for personal growth.

Chapter 4

Put Yourself in the Picture

Bob Jacks

Imagine it's a Friday, but not just any Friday. It's the first Friday of the month, the night our Bible study meets. As I leave my office, I feel a growing sense of anticipation. Last month, one of the members of the study stayed late, and I prayed with him as he committed his life to Jesus Christ. He hopes to bring his sister and brother-in-law to the meeting tonight. Briefly, I wonder about who else might be new at tonight's study and then, as I drive, I silently pray for the meeting and those who will come.

It doesn't just happen . . .

This night will be the culmination of thirty days of prayer, study and planning. Betty and I, and our host couples, have been hard at work to make this a ministry to people, not just an event. Individually and as couples, we have prayed for the members of the study and their specific needs. Two weeks ago, the six of us met together for a potluck dinner and prayer time; we do this every month. Individually, we phoned some of the group members to demonstrate love and offer encouragement. Some of us have also had breakfast or lunch with someone from the study. We use every opportunity we can to further build a relationship or to counsel regarding a need, or perhaps to follow up someone who became a Christian at the study.

Being the leader, I have also been reviewing John 5, our study chapter for tonight. I have taught it many times, but I have been reading and rereading it this past month, prayerfully asking God to guide me to the thoughts and applications that will be most helpful to our present group. I don't keep notes from the previous times I led a discussion. I want the members to enjoy something freshly prepared, so I always prepare a new outline.

As I arrive home and walk in the door, I know what to expect. Betty always prepares a simple supper on these first Fridays. We are a team, and the Bible study is the most important ministry in our lives. We don't want to risk arriving late. We learned long ago that it's important to arrive thirty minutes early to exchange information with the host couples so that all of us can be relaxed and ready to greet and visit with even the earliest arrivals.

Our host couples are equally serious about their commitment. In addition to all of their other prayers and personal contacts, every month they send a postcard reminder to everyone who has attended plus any new contacts. Four or five days before the meeting, they phone each individual or couple. Meeting only once a month requires that degree of diligence or too many would forget.

Everything is in readiness . . .

Our study is meeting at Ken's and Rita's home. As Betty and I drive the 20-mile distance to their home, Rita arranges the coffee and tea pots on the kitchen counter. Ken is in the living room, placing the chairs in a comfortable semi-circle and turning on all the lights. Their final preparation is to tuck away their two wire-haired terriers to the lower level for the evening. Distractions by pets, children or phones can greatly hinder personal ministry in a home study, so they take care to avoid them.

We arrive early. Just being early underscores the importance of this ministry and allows the preparation time essential to being ready and relaxed when our guests arrive. Warm light shows through the windows. The front light makes it easy to find the knocker. Ken welcomes us in. Briefly, we exchange information with one another, learning about any last-minute significant happenings in our lives or the lives of those who will come tonight. We discuss who will be new to the study and who will not be able to come. We have a brief prayer together, but by the time the first guest arrives, we have switched gears. We want the atmosphere light and enthusiastic, not heavy and "spiritual."

The smell of coffee greets people as they enter the room. Some help themselves to a cup, while others prefer to wait until after the study. We talk and joke with one another, meet new people, learn about their interests and engage in relaxed conversation. Betty and I and our host couples make it a point, both before and after the study, not to spend time with each other, but with our guests, helping them to feel at home and trying to be sensitive to any needs they have or what is happening in their lives at the time.

It's time to begin . . .

After about 15 minutes, Ken suggests, "Let's move into the living room." People settle into comfortable chairs or places on the floor and we hand out the paperback Living New Testaments. I welcome the group and give a couple of sentences of orientation to what we will be doing for the benefit of the newcomers. I remind them that we will not discuss church or religion but the relevance of God for our lives today. Then, after putting everyone at ease by assuring them that I will not call upon anyone unless they want to ask a question or make a comment, I announce the page number of the chapter we will study.

I introduce the study, John chapter 5, by telling a little about the author and how much of his writing focuses on individuals who have had a face-to-face encounter with Jesus Christ. I remind them of Nicodemus and the woman at the well in chapters 3 and 4.

For 45 minutes we journey through the fifth chapter of John. The sick man at the Bethesda Pool offers a great opportunity to talk about Jesus' concern for our needs and the importance of wanting help and not being content to live with excuses. I offer as many practical illustrations and applications as I can. I draw heavily upon my own personal experiences and stories about my family, being careful not to say anything that would cause them embarrassment. Using an informal conversational style, I try to keep good eye contact with the group and draw them into the discussion. It's working. Sometimes the atmosphere is more subdued. But not tonight. We talk about God's power to heal our physical bodies and His power to forgive our sins.

All too quickly it's time to close. I say, "It's time for us to end our study and enjoy the refreshments Rita has prepared, but before we do, let me just summarize what we have been talking about." I then review, in the simplest terms I know, how it's possible to know that we have passed from death to life, as the 24th verse of the chapter teaches. I tell the group that if anyone has any further questions, I'll be happy to talk with them while we are having coffee.

Rita slipped out of the room a few minutes early, so the coffee cake and beverages are already on the counter. As the people leave the living room, I hold back, waiting to see if someone wants to take the initiative to talk with me. No one comes immediately, but I notice Betty sitting with a lady who came for the first time. She is living with her second husband and having problems with her 16-year-old daughter who is bitter because her relationship with her step-father isn't good. For the next 20 minutes, Betty becomes better acquainted with the lady and assures her of God's available comfort and guidance. She agrees to come back next month, feeling encouraged by the study and her conversation with Betty.

I join the others in taking refreshments, and our host couples and I individually drift into various areas of the rooms being used and engage in conversation with our guests. It will be unusual if, before the night is over, one or more of us will not have either prayed with someone who wants to become a Christian or had an in-depth conversation regarding knowing Christ personally, as Betty is having with our first-time visitor.

We stay as long as anyone wants to visit. When it's obvious that all of the surfaced needs have been met, we leave, driving home with thanksgiving to

our God Who gives to us, as lay people, this tremendous opportunity to have such a life-changing
ministry in the lives of others.

No, it's not over. It's just beginning. Another
thirty days for follow-up, prayer and inviting. And,
for me, beginning Monday morning, preparing John,
chapter six. I know the Lord will give me new
insights even though I have led a study on this
chapter at least a dozen times.

For further study —
Acts 10:23-43

Urgency and gratitude

Helga

Being willing to host a Bible study in our home was my response to deep feelings of both *urgency and gratitude*.

Urgency, because of the death of someone very close to me. Up until a few years ago, I had taken life for granted. I felt it was here today and would be here tomorrow. But then, all of a sudden, someone I loved was gone. I realized that life was precious, fragile and not something to be taken lightly.

I also had a deep sense of gratitude. When my dad died, the Lord walked through the sorrow with me. If He had not been there, I would have been very bitter and unhappy. I wanted to show my gratitude. Hosting a Bible study was my opportunity.

Even though I had this twofold desire to open my home to ministry, I still felt weak in the knees. Boldness is not one of my strengths, but God promises to make His strength perfect in our weakness (2 Corinthians 12:9). I decided to turn the whole thing over to Him so I could sleep easily and not be upset.

We sent out the written invitations and then prepared to follow up with a phone call. I wrote out what I wanted to say and began dialing the phone. I don't know if the person answering even had an opportunity to say, "hello." I just started reading my invitation. I could hardly believe it when my friend said that she and her husband would like to come.

This experience has given me the excitement of seeing neighbors come to Christ and the joy of seeing them grow. There's something about seeing a new Christian growing that also stimulates your own growth. And I also had the pleasure of making new friends.

Chapter 5

It Takes a Team

Bob Jacks

What will God do through three available couples? We did a little survey on four Bible studies we held in Connecticut. The number of people who became Christians over a two-year period amounted to 15 to 25 in each study.

If that can happen in Connecticut, it can happen anywhere. To say "it can't happen here" is to limit God and the power of His Holy Spirit. So, if you have a couples' study, I think you can generally expect somewhere between 15 to 25 people to receive Christ over a two- to three-year period. And that does not count the reproduction that can come from those lives. Even if the number were half or one-fourth that amount, this would still be an exciting ministry.

If you make no effort, you get no results. From a mathematical standpoint, having just two new Christians out of a study is infinitely better than failing to reach out and having zero new Christians.

Of course, these results don't just happen. Each one of the chapters in this book reveals at least one essential which I believe God will honor to make your ministry fruitful. This chapter is no exception. Choosing the right ministry team is foundational to effective ministry.

Why have a team? Because it is biblical and it is practical. Jesus sent out His disciples to minister in twos. Paul always seemed to have a team, even when he was in prison. He ministered together with Luke, Barnabas, Silas, Timothy and others. There is a strength and encouragement that results from working side by side with another dedicated couple. We become accountable to one another, which helps our commitment. Further, a team allows spiritual gifts to be exercised. Those with the gift of teaching supplement those with the gifts of faith, hospitality and knowing how to relate to others. Couples function together as parts of a body.

A leadership team should consist of three couples: the couple who lead the Bible study; and two couples who host the study, providing the home and the refreshments and doing the primary inviting and follow-up.

Ingredients which every team member must have in common . . .

Being involved in spiritual battle requires being spiritually equipped. This involves even the attitudes of those who are going to be a part of your team. Look for men and women who have a heart for God, a burden for those who do not know Christ and a desire to introduce others to Him.

Add to that the ingredient of prayer. Without prayer, people can go through all the motions without ever seeing the harvest. If leaders are not willing to meet to pray, we suggest they go no further. I advise ministry teams to meet monthly for a time of prayer with a schedule that is relaxed enough to be able to pray specifically for the needs of each person and group.

Our dependence is upon the fullness (empowerment) of the Holy Spirit. This is not a muscle ministry, but a ministry of the Lord. Each leader must be filled with and controlled by the Holy Spirit because to work as a team effectually requires power and harmony that only the Spirit can give.

Along with these spiritual qualities, there is the need for just plain faithfulness and dedication to a local church. This ministry is built on relationships, and this requires faithful attendance and follow-through. Leaders must work to develop meaningful relationships with group members. It doesn't just happen.

Even though Bible study leaders deliberately avoid promoting their church when conducting the study, the church is an essential ingredient. It provides the nurture, supervision and accountability for the leaders of the study. It also offers the breadth of teaching and fellowship every Christian needs to grow properly. The bridge to a church for a new Christian in your study must be crossed sensitively, but it must be crossed, and leaders who are committed to a local church will assure that it does happen.

The role of the host couples . . .

Whether you call it the gift of hospitality or just loving people and enjoying being with them, nothing confirms the reality of the message of the Christ we proclaim like an outgoing love. Such love should radiate from the host couples. Such love motivates host couples to be willing to work behind the scenes.

Host couples carry the prime responsibility for planning a list of potential members to launch the group and then inviting them to come. Hosts should ask the Lord to influence them as they think of names of people to invite. They may hesitate to approach some of these people, but should invite them anyway and never stop inviting.

As a study matures, it may move to the home of one of the members, but initially, one of the host couples usually provides the home. The same transition usually occurs in the responsibility to provide refreshments. The host couples may furnish the food at the beginning, but involving other members later helps to establish their commitment to the study and to make it their own.

The host couples maintain regular contact with people who become a part of the group to build relationships, or to follow up on a need in their lives.

Normally, the couples' studies meet only once a month, so a thorough approach to reminding people is a necessity. It is good for the host couples to call every member about one week before. At the leaders' discretion, they may need to call some or all of the members of the study again on the night preceding the study. An ideal approach is to send a reminder card a week to ten days before the meeting, then follow up with the call.

The hosts encourage group members to bring others. As people in the study become Christians, they will begin to invite friends. This is an important facet to develop because new Christians have so many established relationships with non-Christians that make it easy to reach out to them.

Following up new Christians includes arranging personal visits, making phone calls, giving appropriate follow-up materials . . . whatever helps to ground and encourage new Christians in their faith.

Finally, host couples work closely with the other members of their leadership team and those of other groups. They participate in the monthly team prayer meeting and work on special events, quarterly or semi-annually.

The role of leaders . . .

Leaders, too, must know how to communicate to non-Christians, but they practice this more in the group setting than in one-to-one relationships.

Their skill must be one of leading without lecturing. They must be able to relate the message of God's Word to people with little or no church experience and knowledge of the Bible. The emphasis should be on salvation and growth experiences for the new Christian, helping people think their way to a commitment.

The leader needs to have the dedication to spend the necessary time in preparation to be effective. For a study to be effective, it must be kept simple. To be simple is often the most difficult task of leading.

While the host couples assume the primary responsibility for follow-up, the leader joins them in bearing responsibility for group members between meetings. His visible role often makes him uniquely qualified for relating to people and dealing with individual needs.

In relating to his other team members, the leader provides training so the host couples will be able to do their jobs well. Other responsibilities include conducting the monthly prayer meetings and working on special events, quarterly or semi-annually.

Resources to do the job . . .

If these responsibilities seem awesome, this may be a good time to review God's promises in Chapter Three, "Thoughts for Winning."

God has not left us without resources. We do have the power of the Holy Spirit, God's Word and prayer. As the Lord stirs your heart with the impulse to demonstrate and share His love with others through Bible studies, you can be convinced of His enabling strength.

For further study —
Acts 16:1-10

I began to see a difference
Hal

Ever since I can remember, I have had an unbelievable appetite for competitive sports. During my high school and college years, sports were my total life. During my senior year in college, I was drafted by a major league baseball team, but physical problems ended that career prematurely.

I started a career in sales which became extremely good. My marriage was also good, but as in most marriages, not without some rough spots. My wife began attending a Bible study in our neighborhood and would try to share with me some of the concepts which she had learned there. I felt the group was good for her, but saw no need in my life for anything relating to God.

When I met some of the people who hosted and led some of the Bible studies, my attitude changed and I began to attend. Soon, I began playing with the church's softball team. Some of the men in the Bible study participated.

I began to see a difference in their attitude towards the world and people. I realized the difference between their attitude and mine was a result of knowing Christ in a personal way. I later invited Christ into my life, and He has enhanced my marriage tremendously and helped me start my own business, which continues to prosper under His leadership.

Chapter 6

Beginning

Betty Jacks

Set a date and begin!

Beginning is the most likely area where all of us are prone to seek special help — some fore-discovered solution to make this most difficult part of the entire strategy easy.

This book is designed to help you do the study right. Nevertheless, you can do a great many things wrong and still have a measure of success. God honors His Word and our obedience. He will not allow Himself to be placed in a box as though there were only one way He can do His work in people's lives. But one thing is sure, there cannot be any success *unless you begin*.

Most Christians have a desire to reach out to families and friends. As you read these pages, you may have thought, "This may work for me." Your heart may even be beating a little faster as you think of the potential, yet fear grips you. That is 100% natural. We often say if you are not a little scared, you really don't understand.

When Bob and I were faced with the claims of Christ, we knew a commitment was required and put it off. You will find the same tendency to put off starting a Bible study. You will never start unless you set a date. That is the commitment — the date. Set it.

I had always said I could not lead this type of study. I babysat, hosted and supported Bob as he led for years. Then, four years ago, a group of women agreed to a women's study as a result of a film we had at our church. We made a list of those who were not from our church and decided to start a small outreach group. But we had no leader. My husband said, "I guess you're it." I resisted. I had led a couple of studies for Christians through the years, but I was scared. Finally, I realized God was calling me. I committed. You, too, must commit.

Give yourself two to four months lead time so you will have adequate opportunity to plan, prepare your ministry team and invite others. This will help assure an in-depth ministry. Then, once you have established your launch date, stick to it!

Finding the People . . .

Where do the people for the study come from? Answer: Anywhere you can find them.

The important thing is to look for non-Christians.

There is a great temptation to invite your church friends because we like to think numbers equal success. However, your study will be effective in reaching others for Christ to the extent you keep it simple and geared to the participants' needs. If there are many Christians in the study, you lose that needed simplicity. As a matter of fact, you could lose the study.

Sometimes, after a study is in progress, the members themselves will invite others and some may be Christians. You need to be sensitive, but avoid letting anyone who is looking for a more in-depth study change the direction of your group. This may require your talking with them personally.

You can begin with a home event . . .

Host couples should first pray and then make a list of neighbors, friends, relatives, those with whom they work. A potluck dinner or dessert in a home can launch a study group.

Your invitation could read:

> Please come to our home for a potluck dinner on Friday, September 30, at 7:00 P.M. After dinner we will have a discussion on "The Reality of Christianity in Today's World." The discussion will be led by Bob Smith, Field Manager with the Wilson Company.
>
> We do hope that you can come. I'll phone you in a couple of days to confirm and to see what you would like to bring.

For this kind of meeting, we always invite two to three times more people than our home will accommodate. Normally, there will be that much attrition. But if you should have an unusually large response, wouldn't it be great to have the problem of creatively accommodating all the people? In our couples' studies, it is not unusual for people to be sitting on the floor or on stairs leading out of the room. That kind of a crowd only brings added enthusiasm.

Or build on the foundation
of a women's study . . .

Actually, at the very beginning, while we were
procrastinating in starting our first couples' study, a
friend of mine and I started a women's study. From
that group we gleaned many of the husband and
wife teams for our first couples' study. Don't overlook
this strategic resource.

Often, women come to know Christ, but have
no comfortable place to expose their husbands to
what they have come to believe. A friend's living
room is an ideal place, a friendly atmosphere, with
non-threatening paperback Bibles. No formality, no
organ, no order of service and no collection. This
is freedom for the non-believer.

Or follow special events . . .

Another great way to launch a home Bible study
is following a special event at your church which
attracts visitors — a film series, family life speaker,
Fourth of July picnic, special holiday program, parents' night for Vacation Bible School or whatever
unique opportunity you might have in your church.

Either at the home potluck or in a special church
meeting, you could announce the study by saying:

We're planning to launch a monthly home
Bible study group where we can learn more
about how to better relate to God and to others
in our daily lives.

This is an informal group where all you have
to do is come. You don't have to bring anything
and you don't have to enter the discussion
unless you want to. We won't be discussing

various religions or denominations. We'll just be talking about what the Bible has to say to help us meet the challenges of living and relating to others.

I'm going to ask all of you to fill out the cards we are passing out to let us know if you are interested in coming or if you would like us to call you to tell you more about it.

Sample Card

Name			
First	Last		Spouse

Address _____

City, State, Zip _____

Home phone _____

Work phone _____

Please check appropriate boxes:

☐ Yes, ☐ I ☐ we would be interested in attending a monthly Home Bible Study.

☐ Please call ☐ me ☐ us to tell me/us more about it.

☐ Sorry, ☐ I ☐ we will not be able to be involved at this time.

When making this invitation, I am sure to allow sufficient time and not rush this part of the meeting. Everyone completes a card and then we collect them all. This allows the ones who are interested to feel more comfortable, and we receive a more positive response.

Also, we promptly and thoroughly follow through on every positive response. Generally, the interest of the people is higher immediately after the meeting. It may decline if we wait too long.

Notice that the wording of the response card allows people to say "no" graciously, but does not rule out the possibility of your contacting them at a later time. So we are sure to keep their names. When the study is in progress, we can give them a friendly call to see if they would like to come. Or, we can contact them when new studies are formed.

As we contact and invite people to a study, we try to be relaxed. If we are uptight, they may tend to be defensive or withdrawn. On the other hand, they will respond to genuine warmth and friendliness.

For further study —
Romans 10:1-13

Overwhelmed with the warmth and friendship

Ken

My wife attended a film series at a church not far from where she was working and filled out a card indicating she was interested in attending a home Bible study. When she received a phone invitation to a couples' study, she called me at my office. I was apprehensive, not sure what to expect, but I agreed to go.

The day came and I was very nervous. I wondered what it would be like and what kind of people would be there. I dreaded the possibility that the meeting would be heavily "religious." The fear of the unknown was devastating.

Sitting in that living room, my wife and I were *overwhelmed with the warmth and friendship* of the "regular" people we met. The leader was very open and relaxed and made us feel the same. He told us we didn't have to join in the discussion unless we wanted to . . . that we were not going to talk about specific religions or denominations . . . that we would just study the Bible and try to understand and learn from it.

At the time, I was going through a career change. I was leaving my position of ten years as vice-president of a small furniture manufacturing company. There were a lot of decisions to make and I was concerned.

What the leader said about committing one's life to Christ was very appealing and a lot of the discussion was really hitting home. About the third month, when we were studying John 3, the leader gave an opportunity for us to ask Christ into our lives. And I did. It seemed that all my burdens and frustrations came to an end. I had peace.

I began to learn to trust Christ for practical daily decisions, and the pieces of my life began to fall into place. The changes in me and our home have been fantastic. And now we have the privilege of hosting a Bible study of our own.

I wonder if any of this would have happened if we had not felt so completely at home at that first study.

Chapter 7

Focusing on Needs

Bob Jacks

Plan any kind of Bible study and look at the resource you have for meeting needs:

> The whole Bible was given to us by inspiration from God and is useful to teach us what is true and to make us realize what is wrong in our lives; it straightens us out and helps us do what is right. It is God's way of making us well prepared at every point, fully equipped to do good to everyone (2 Timothy 3:16,17).

> For whatever God says to us is full of living power: it is sharper than the sharpest dagger, cutting swift and deep into our innermost thoughts and desires with all their parts, exposing us for what we really are (Hebrews 4:12).

> Forever, O Lord, your Word stands firm in heaven (Psalm 119:89).

For greatness' sake . . .

With promises like those above, every Bible study should be meaningful. Often the difference between a *good* Bible study and a *great* Bible study is sharply focusing on your purpose and limiting yourself to your target audience.

I do all I can to avoid creating a "churchy" atmosphere that would be a barrier to clear and effective communication. I try to be spontaneous and light and avoid becoming rigid and proper.

Most of us who have been Christians for some time have an obscure sense of how many non-Christians feel:

- "My needs are paramount."
- "It's not fun to go to church or a religious activity."
- "Aggressive Christians threaten me."
- "When I'm with Christians, I have a feeling of being on the outside of things."

A beginning point for meeting needs is to appreciate the attitudes and feelings of the people you are trying to reach. Then design your study to eliminate every possible barrier. It takes a willingness to unlearn any attitudes or actions which set you apart. You want to remove obstacles and reach out to them in a comfortable way for them.

When my sons go fishing, they use all kinds of equipment and subtle ways to entice the fish to bite. Christ said that if we follow Him, He will make us to be fishers of men. Using subtle ways to create a positive environment to win others to Christ is not being deceptive. It is being wise and loving people enough to be sensitive to their feelings and needs rather than forcing your own style on them. We call this S.P. (Spiritual Planning). It is what Matthew did when He prepared a great feast as a setting to present Jesus to a large group of people (Luke 5:27-32).

Often, people come and are literally stiff, especially the husbands of wives who are new Christians and are now trying to interest their husbands. It is not unusual to have a husband who is a salesman or Sales Manager come with cold, clammy and often sweaty hands, scared stiff. My goal becomes to get them comfortable, to be relaxed.

One way to do this, in a couples' study, is to provide an inexpensive modern language translation of the New Testament for everyone. Most non-Christian people would not want to be seen by their friends while carrying a Bible. In one study, a woman came carrying her Bible in a brown paper bag. To her, it was an embarrassment to be seen toting a Bible.

Here are some suggestions:

Do . . .

1. Make people comfortable.
2. Provide ash trays. Remember, this is not a prayer meeting. This is evangelism.
3. Before the study, talk about things they are interested in — football, antiques, weather, their jobs, etc.
4. Take the phone off the hook or have someone nearby to answer it.
5. Include people in conversation. None of your leadership team should ever be in the same place at the same time.
   Separate and involve more of your guests in comfortable conversation.
6. Be sensitive to timid or turned-off people. Include them in casual conversation before and after the study.
7. Provide a copy of a modern translation for each person there, the same copy you use yourself. You can direct them to a specific location by referring to page numbers first and then telling them where to look on the

page. Many non-Christians would not be able to locate books of the Bible. For example, you could say, "Tonight we'll start our study on page number 162 where we find chapter 10 of the Book of John."

8. Encourage people to take the Bible home.
9. Be sensitive to time. Limit your Bible study to forty-five minutes or one hour maximum.
10. Cover all of the material planned, even if you summarize.
11. Prepare yourself to love people rather than trying to force theology on them.

Don't . . .

1. Pray, unless it is a sentence prayer for the refreshments.
2. Play religious music.
3. Talk about religion or your church.
4. Clique with your friends.
5. Talk to others in a whisper.
6. Berate, or even discuss, religious groups.
7. Ask people to read aloud.
8. Call on people by name, unless they have indicated they have a question or comment.
9. Invite your pastor.
10. Make it "churchy."

My goal is to do everything I can to make sure that the people will come back again. As they keep returning to the study, they are more and more exposed to the Word of God and the power of the Holy Spirit expressed through the atmosphere in

the home and the love reflected in the lives of the
leadership couples.

**For further study —
John 4:1-19**

Let's stop looking for a harvest

*Pastor John**

Study the Bible and church history and you find again and again that the gospel has always spread most effectively through a home situation. Within each home is a family network, and from each family member a web of relationships reaches to every area of community life. What better way to reach to others with the message of Jesus Christ than to begin in our homes and work through our webs of relationships?

I often challenge people to take a red pencil and underline all of the commands to witness in the writings of the apostle Paul. If you wanted to do this, do you know how many you would find? None. Not a single one.

Why? I believe it was because reaching out to others was a natural part of the Christian life. As Christians, we live in daily contact with non-Christians. In those relationships, the life we have in Christ should be overflowing so others are drawn to know Him, too.

Let's stop looking for a harvest and realize the harvest is already here, on our doorsteps. It's the people who live around you, those with whom you work, other friends and acquaintances. Bring them into the comfort of your home to hear a non-threatening presentation of the truth of the Bible and see how ripe that harvest is.

As the pastor of a church who believes in the church, I am excited about this form of ministry. It doesn't take place within the four walls of our church, but it's as much a part of our ministry as anything we do. We train and provide leadership. We pray and encourage the workers. And we nurture and help sustain the fruit of the harvest.

The challenge for any pastor and congregation will be to allow this ministry to function as a separate entity while still providing the guidance and continuity needed. Tie it too closely to the church and it loses its attractiveness to the very people you want to win. Divorce it from the church and you rob it of resources essential to maximum effectiveness. It's a fine line, but it can be followed; it must be followed.

* Rev. John Peterson is Senior Pastor of the Avon Community Baptist Church, where Bob and Betty Jacks are members.

Chapter 8

Your Pastor's Role

Bob Jacks

Because of where we live and the negative attitude of many people regarding the organized church, we have a rule that pastors don't attend our evangelistic home Bible studies. For seven years, my own pastor has had a desire to attend one of our studies, but we have agreed together that he should not come. He is well known in our community and I know that if people in the study recognized him, it would inhibit discussion.

Does this sound overly rigid and arbitrary? Perhaps. But consider the implications. What kind of climate are we trying to create? A totally non-church and non-threatening atmosphere. Our goal is not to force the non-Christians in attendance to have to make allowances for us. We are going all the way in our efforts to meet them on their territory.

What would the presence of someone known to be a pastor do to that objective? The answer is obvious. Just one person saying something like, "Hi, Pastor John," would immediately raise red flags.

People there would at least think, "Is this a church group?"

How do pastors feel about this? I'm sure there are a variety of responses. Some may be threatened. I wish all shared the attitude of my own pastor. He said, "You *have* to do it that way."

Of course, there are always exceptions. We have had other pastors come to observe for a night, but we have not introduced them as pastors. In larger meetings, and if they understand the atmosphere you want to create, they can lose themselves in the crowd. You will have to be the final judge of how to include your pastor.

Of the church, but not in the church . . .

When you begin a program like this, most pastors and leaders want to tie it more and more to the local church. This is where tension could come. Is this evangelistic home Bible study a part of the church?

If you say "yes," there is a problem. Tie it too closely to the church and you neutralize its effectiveness in reaching the raw, non-churched person you are trying to win. It must maintain its own identity *out there* in the world where the non-Christian lives. Remember, you are fishing in the deep.

If you say "no," you have another problem. The Bible study needs a structure to support it and nurture it. You don't want its success and longevity to rest upon one person or a couple. If a ministry is worthwhile, you want to feed it and provide for its continuance. This is what the church is uniquely called and equipped to do, to disciple and train men and women for ministry.

Further, you want to conserve the fruit of the Bible studies. They are effective in introducing men and women to Jesus Christ, and they do provide an immediate follow-up. The studies function best, however, when those won to Christ are left just a little hungry. Their spiritual appetite helps to draw them into a local church fellowship.

Some may already have a church home. If it is a church where they can be fed and nourished and helped to grow, great, we let them stay there. If it is a church that is not equipped to satisfy their spiritual hunger, they will seek growth elsewhere, perhaps in our church. We have seen this happen time and time again.

Sometimes a link to our church has been established by arranging counseling with one of our pastors for people who have deep needs and no church home. As situations arise, trust the Holy Spirit for wisdom in knowing what will be best for each individual or couple. Then be responsible to do your part in either discipling them further or "letting go."

Perhaps the best definition is that the home Bible study should be a ministry *of* the church, but *not identified with* the church. *Of the church,* to provide trained leadership, continuity and follow-up for new Christians. *Not identified with the church,* to assure there are no barriers to reaching the most diversified audience possible.

I believe the pastor should have confidence in his Bible study leaders and spend time with them. A pastor can't go and check the study out. He must believe in his leaders or he will develop vain imaginations. Only by spending time with his leaders will he develop the confidence to train them and then trust them for this ministry.

Of course, there is also a responsibility for the Bible study leaders. While not promoting their church, they must be totally committed to it. The church provides their own spiritual nourishment.

Also, their ministry will be superficial if new Christians do not ultimately become a part of a church family.

Keeping the cutting edge . . .

Another responsibility of the pastor is to help the groups maintain their cutting edge. In almost every discipleship and evangelism group, it is the rare leader who will not tend to drop what is most important to keep.

In an evangelistic home Bible study, there are key ingredients to guard: the emphasis on prayer, the personal contact with group members between meetings and follow-up. Involved pastors can help leaders maintain these crucial ingredients.

There is one additional area where the pastor is so important to this outreach. When people from the Bible studies receive Christ and come to your church, what will they find? Does your church have a positive identity in the community? Are your people warm? Do you have ministries within your church that will meet the needs of these new Christians? There must be a total mix to make this ministry work. No person's role is more important and effective than that of a pastor with the right attitude, non-threatened and involved in the leaders' lives.

Following these parameters, I believe it would not be unusual to find about one-fourth to one-half of the converts from the Bible studies ending up in your church. This has been our experience. I believe this is an outstanding success rate.

For further study —
Ephesians 4:11-16

I was able to absorb the basics

Kevin

I was dragged into church every now and then as a child. As I got older and went to high school and college, I was totally nonplused by the idea of God.

Philosophical discussions roused my interest, but I couldn't understand how people who seemed otherwise quite rational and well-balanced could believe in this poppycock about a risen Lord.

Little did I realize how my attitude toward the message of Christ was going to change. While I was in college an emptiness began to creep into my life. I sought ways to fill that void and was never at a loss for new things to try . . . marriage . . . a new home . . . a car . . . a job change . . . every one an empty pursuit.

I became a police officer. The rigors of the job and the emotional drain resulted in my wife and I drifting apart and, eventually, the final curtain on our marriage. It also put me into the world of desperate people and high stakes. I was tired and bored and just didn't know what I wanted to do.

While going downhill with no end in sight, I married my present wife, Nancy. We were both floundering, but we deeply loved each other.

One day Nan announced that she was going to a Bible study. I was concerned because I feared she was becoming involved with some kind of cult. She went and returned, telling me about the clarity and simplicity of the message she was hearing and encouraging me to attend, also.

Over a period of three or four studies, *I was able to absorb the basics* of the gospel of our Lord Jesus Christ and I came to the place where I accepted Him as my Savior.

I know that God has many ways to bring people to Himself. But I was a person totally opposed to the church and religion, who just dared people to try to talk me out of my position. There probably could not have been a more effective tool than that home Bible study to provide the opportunity for me to consider and respond to the claims of Jesus Christ.

Chapter 9

Leading the Study

Bob Jacks

The Gospel of John is ideally suited to an evangelistic home Bible study.* The purpose of the book is presented in John 20:30,31:

> Jesus' disciples saw him do many other miracles besides the ones told about in this book, but these are recorded so that you will believe that he is the Messiah, the Son of God, and that believing in him you will have life.

This is the recurring theme of John. As one of the Bible study leaders from my church observed, every chapter of John has the same message, "believing in Jesus Christ." Only the characters change.

Studying one chapter each month provides an excellent opportunity, every time you meet, to tell your group about Jesus and how to become a Christian. Initially, this is your prime objective. That's not complicated, but it does require preparation. You are

---

* Alternate methods are discussed in chapter 12.

leading non-Christians who may be unchurched and unlearned in spiritual truth. Because you want to relate to your group according to their interests and needs, you will need to prepare thoroughly for each lesson.

Be relevant . . .

I find it important to identify themes that will arouse the interest of our group. We discuss ideas that are relevant to them and help them make applications to their lives and problems. And when I explain how to become a Christian, I do so in a simple, clear and concise way; straightforward, but casual and relaxed. This encourages the group to feel relaxed and have more freedom to respond.

In leading your group, you can stimulate them through a variety of approaches. Sometimes you may want to review the entire chapter of John you are studying that week. Sometimes you may select a part of the chapter or only a few verses, do a character study or identify and study key thoughts. No matter what you do, always use the same careful planning and creativity in explaining how a person can become a Christian.

I begin my preparation with prayer, asking Christ what He would have me share with my group during the next lesson.

Be thorough . . .

After praying, I read the passage again and again. If I lead a study using John 3 on Friday, then I'll start reading John 4 the following Monday, so I can saturate my mind with the content for a whole month. I need to allow the Holy Spirit to give me good illustrations during the month from my own personal experience or material I read.

I find it necessary to prepare in a quiet place, without being rushed or interrupted. Then I begin putting my thoughts on paper. As I write, I decide my major objective and how to organize the passage into easily handled parts — paragraphs, ideas, character studies, or whatever.

Though I use several modern language translations, a commentary and a Bible dictionary to prepare, I limit the amount of materials I take to the study. I find it best to have only a few notes on a single sheet of paper or three by five card. This gives a tremendous amount of freedom.

The nature of this study makes it important that you not be tied to your materials. It's imperative to be free to relate to the group with good eye contact and sensitivity to how they are responding.

One helpful tool is a flip chart. It's easily transportable and unique enough to draw people's attention. The simple diagrams I use aid learning.

For example, I remember the diagram I drew which resulted in Rosalie becoming a Christian.

1 Thessalonians 4:16-18

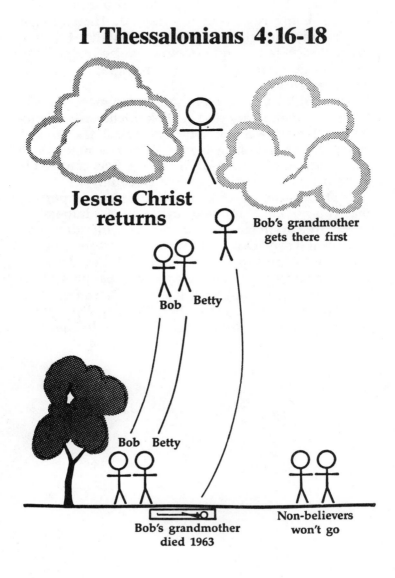

I explained that while we are in Connecticut, my grandmother is lying in a grave in the hills of West Virginia. But my Bible tells me a day is coming when we — my wife, our children, and I — are going to be "caught up...to meet the Lord in the air" (1 Thessalonians 4:17). My grandmother will, too, and we will be together again. Only those who are not believers will be left behind. This truth, pictured by this simple drawing, communicated to Rosalie, as nothing had over the previous two years, the night she put her faith in Christ.

Don't worry. After you have done what is humanly possible for a successful study, you can then leave the results to God. He knows the needs of the group. He has the power to meet those needs. Pray and trust Him to work through you and, by His Holy Spirit, meet the needs of each member.

I never keep notes. I have probably taught the Gospel of John about a dozen times over the past fifteen years. The reason I don't keep notes is that I would be tempted to rely on them instead of preparing a fresh message.

This not only sharpens me, but also allows for the Lord to communicate a different message for my present group than He had for the last one. God will also give you the message that He thinks is important. The Holy Spirit will make you sensitive to what should be communicated because He knows your group better than you do.

Off to a good start . . .

To establish the right atmosphere at the beginning of the study, I'll often say something like this:

We're not here to learn a lot of details about the Bible; we're here to learn more about the character of God and how He can work in our lives today.

That's refreshing to people. To them, it's important to understand God's love and how to experience it. And, by letting them know I am not going to ask questions to test their knowledge of the Bible, they can relax and listen and learn.

Then I may introduce the study by saying:

John was written by one of the twelve apostles. He was one of the three closest men to Christ, and he knew Christ very intimately. Now, the Book of John is a little different from the first three gospels. He tells a little bit more about one-to-one contacts that Christ had. As a matter of fact, tonight we're going to be studying about the one-to-one contact Jesus had with a woman at the well and what that conversation was all about.

I talk about these real-life situations. You can take every one of these contacts Christ had with people and relate them to people today.

I also tell people ahead of time:

I'm going to do all of the reading. I'm not going to ask any of you to read, and I won't ask any of you to make comments unless you want to. Also, if you have any questions, be sure to bring them up.

Everyone has been given the same edition of the New Testament. I like to use the Living New Testament for its simplicity and ease of reading and understanding. Because each member has the same edition, I don't have to locate the place where we will be studying by chapter and verse; I can just say, "Turn to page 116 ."

Encourage participation . . .

A natural fear in leading a study of this kind is that people will ask questions for which we have no answers. That fear, I believe, is one of Satan's choice obstacles to having a meaningful and fruitful study.

You need to encourage comments and questions from your group. That's the secret to keeping your study from being theoretical and making it practical. You need to know what the group members are thinking so that you can apply the passage to their life situations.

Encourage as much participation as you can, but without calling on people individually. Your members need to have the security of knowing they will never be called upon, never embarrassed by having to parade their ignorance. Your goal is an open atmosphere that says the only dumb question is one which isn't asked. Let there be complete freedom of expression.

Your questions should encourage thought. Questions like:

- What do you think this passage means?
- What does this passage tell us about God?
- What does it say about us?
- How do you think you could apply the truth of this passage in your life this week?
- What does this passage mean to you?
- What do you think God would want you to learn from this passage?
- Can any of you identify with this person?
- Have any of you had an experience similar to the one described in this passage?

You can expect spiritually inaccurate responses to your questions.

> The man who isn't a Christian can't understand and can't accept these thoughts from God, which the Holy Spirit teaches us. They sound foolish to him, because only those who have the Holy Spirit within them can understand what the Holy Spirit means. Others just can't take it in (1 Corinthians 2:14).

Don't worry about that. Every response is a window through which you can see what is in the life of the person. You're learning their thinking, what's bothering them, what their needs are. Every response is an opportunity for you to lead more accurately.

In a sense, when you just lead a group through the passage, you are using a shotgun. You know your target is out there in the shrubbery. You're aiming in the general direction, but that's the best you can do. When people respond to you, suddenly your target is out in the open. You can lay down your shotgun, pick up your rifle and aim for a bullseye.

Keeping participation positive . . .

The only negative side to people asking questions is an inappropriate response, so keep a few simple guidelines in mind.

Never register shock. Whatever a person says, treat his or her comment in a casual, normal way. Your group members must know you accept them just as they are.

Try to say something positive. You can always say something like, "That's a good question" or, "That's an interesting idea." Certainly, you shouldn't embarrass the person by saying, "No, that's not right."

You may want to throw the question out to the group for other responses. Many times the general discussion of the group will clarify the right answer so plainly that you will never have to make an issue over a wrong response.

Consider rewording the question. This often helps to lead the group to an appropriate response.

When leading a group discussion it's also important to:

Respond to people by their names if you can remember them. Say, "Good thought, Bill." In the beginning, you may want to use name tags. At one Bible study we led, the host couple wrote the first name of each person on a piece of masking tape and stuck it on the refrigerator door, so they were available as the members arrived.

Look at people intently when they are talking to you. For you, what they are saying is the most important thing happening in the world at that time. Don't look at your notes or Bible while they are talking. They need to know you are interested.

If you don't know the answer, say so. From your viewpoint, that may be the most negative thing that could happen. From the viewpoint of the group, it is probably the most positive thing. Through your general leading you will have established your role. You will have affirmed clearly enough that you can speak with authority on how to know God. But for your group to know you don't have "all the answers" helps to place you on their level. This will help members relate to you and respond to what you are saying.

If you don't know the answer, you can always say, "I don't know. I really don't know." You can ask if anyone else has ideas about the answer. And you can offer to look up the answer and tell them the next time you meet, or ask someone in the group to look up the answer.

You may suggest that each member of the group try to find the answer before the next study. If you do, be sure to give an opportunity for people to share what they have found at the next meeting.

Don't waste time on foolish questions. Questions like, "Where did Cain get his wife?" serve no useful purpose in this study. You can simply state that you don't know the answer and then refocus the group on the things God has clearly taught in His Word, the things He wants us to know.

Never argue.

Relate to your members in love. Remember, "Love goes on forever" (1 Corinthians 13:8).

The priority of love . . .

That last point, "Relate to your members in love," is undoubtedly most important. It is the love of Christ working through the team and God's Word that wins people. The love chapter of the Bible, 1 Corinthians 13, closes with the words, "There are three things that remain — faith, hope and love — and the greatest of these is love."

I remember a few years ago when a woman made a commitment to Christ in a women's Bible study and said, "I wish my husband could hear this."

The hostess, Arlene, said, "Well, why don't you invite him to the couples' study?"

The woman said, "Oh, my gosh, you don't know my husband. He would never come to something like this."

So we began to pray for her husband, Joe. We all prayed, believing he would come. He was an impossible situation. Totally impossible. There was no way he would ever come to a Bible study. He was a Chester, Pennsylvania, cop, on the force for 35 or 40 years. He had a burr haircut, was a former professional boxer, and had every bad attitude that ever existed toward people.

His wife didn't even have enough nerve to ask her husband to the study. So after about three months of praying, she began sharing with Joe some of the things she had learned in the Bible study. He said, "I just can't believe all the things you're telling me."

She said, "Why don't you come?"

His response was, "OK, I'd just like to come and see what these kooks look like."

He came, and I'll never forget that night. He sat right in front of me with his arms folded and a "show me" attitude. And he made negative comments about everything and everybody. He always had a negative judgment. He was tough.

But the people in the study just began to love the guy and he didn't know how to handle it. This went on for about six months and, slowly, we began to see him soften.

But it was about the ninth month when he finally came to me and asked, "Could I say something at this study?" I told him he could, and he got up and apologized to all the people. He was changed. Christ had transformed his life. The Bible study members had loved him into a personal relationship with Jesus Christ.

He began to share his love for Christ with others in his family. Later, Joe became critically ill and died of cancer. Someday, we'll see Joe. But what if we had not prayed for him and what if his wife had not invited him to the study?

**For further study —
1 John 4:7-21**

It all came together for me

Rita

At one point in my life, I had accomplished a very important career goal. Having just about everything I had ever wanted, I still felt empty. There was a void that I tried to fill with different things, but not Jesus.

I had a religious upbringing and believed in God. Yet, I feared Him and felt He was far away, someplace called "heaven," a place I had doubts of ever getting to.

I refused my mother's attempts to bring me to a Bible study she was attending and continued in my emptiness while she continued to pray for my husband and me.

I contemplated seeing a fortune-teller, someone who could tell me about the future. That's how desperately I was searching for answers. I attended a film series at the church of a colleague of mine. The films inspired me, and after one of them I signed a card indicating I would like to attend a home Bible study, never thinking I would be called. But they did call, and my husband and I did attend.

During the second study, John Chapter 2 was discussed. *It all came together for me.* During the coffee break I spoke with the leader, and he guided me in praying to ask Jesus Christ into my life. The leader and his wife continued a close relationship with us, encouraging us in our growth and later in hosting a Bible study in our home.

Priorities have changed and my outlook is different. I still have struggles and disappointments, but I am not alone with them. I'm so thankful for the long term care and concern of others that first helped bring me to Christ and now encourages my daily walk with Him.

Chapter 10

Following Through

Bob Jacks

One of the greatest strengths of this Bible study concept is the evolving relationship that develops between leaders and each member. When inviting people to the study, leaders get to know them, introduce them to Jesus Christ and, ultimately, help to establish them as disciples.

A web of relationships . . .

There is a web of relationships upon which studies are built. This web contributes greatly to conserving the results.

Some people come into a study group by signing a response card at a special event such as a film or special speaker. Many come by a personal invitation extended by one of the host couples. They come because they already have a relationship with the host person or couple. In either event, host couples can strengthen relationships from month to month as the study meets and as they faithfully make contact with the members by phone and in person between meetings. The result: strong bonds of friendship, most often even before the person may make a commitment to Christ. When this relationship exists, imagine the ease of following through and helping the newly committed Christian to grow spiritually.

Often, it is difficult to follow up new Christians after an evangelistic event or city-wide crusade because they are reluctant to come to your church or even discuss their recent decision. They have no ties. The obstacle of coming as strangers is just too great.

Following this Bible study approach, every new Christian is already on a trail leading back to your church, and they feel good about it because they feel good about the people who have led them to Christ. When they arrive at your church, familiar faces welcome them and introduce them to others.

In large measure, this is a relational evangelism strategy. The leader must have the gift of teaching and may or may not have strong relational skills. The host couples must have these relational skills and pursue personal involvement with those invited and attending a home study.

Relate over coffee . . .

Normally, I close our meeting by announcing that, while we're having coffee, I will be happy to visit with anyone who has a question about the study we just completed. Or, if I closed with an invitation to receive Christ and gave the people an opportunity to invite Christ into their lives, I may ask them to come to me during the refreshment time to tell me about it. Or, I may say something like:

I know this is a decision you're going to want to make. When you do, be sure to tell me about it. Call me, even if it's three o'clock in the morning.

(Two people have actually done that.)

At other times I may make no verbal announcement, but just remain off to the side during the refreshment time so others will feel free to approach me.

I remember when Rita invited Jesus Christ into her life. She had come to the study for the first time the previous month. At the door, her husband and she had introduced themselves by saying, "Hi, we're Ken and Rita. We understand you're starting a Bible study. We want you to know that we're searching, but we're not sure if we're going to be interested in this or not." They were a beautiful couple in their early thirties and had just driven 35 minutes to get to the study.

The night of the study, I remember having told Betty that God was impressing me that someone at the study that night would trust Christ as Savior. I tucked a couple of booklets explaining the gospel into my pocket (as I normally do) and off we went to the study.

After I had finished leading, we all went into the kitchen for the refreshments. But in my heart I prayed, "Well, Lord, if there's somebody here who wants to meet You tonight, I'm going to go back into the living room and it's Your responsibility to get that person back in there."

I went into the living room and Rita followed me. "You know," she said, "you said a couple of things tonight that I really want to ask you about."

I had the Holy Spirit discernment that this could be the person. I made a couple of comments and then said, "Rita, we're talking about a personal relationship with Christ. Can you remember a time when you invited Jesus Christ to come into your life?"

She said, "Well, I'm not exactly sure the way you mean it."

About 80% of the time, people will respond, "I'm not exactly sure." That means "no."

So I replied, "Well, maybe you don't quite understand. Let me read through this little booklet with you and see if I can clear it up." After reading through a simple presentation on how to become a Christian, I asked if she could think of any reason why she would not want to receive Christ right then. She said, "no." We prayed together and she invited Christ into her life.

Afterwards, I challenged her to tell one person what she had done. That was the beginning of an exciting chain of events. She became a vital witness at her work. Her husband, Ken, soon became a Christian, and now they are hosting their own home Bible study in which fourteen people have become Christians in just eight months.

Not only the leader and his wife, but the host couples should also be alert to what group members say during the Bible study and the refreshment time following. All three couples on the team should be involved in follow-up.

Arrange special meeting times . . .

If someone indicates a need or problem, a member of the team should call them or make arrangements to meet with them personally. He or she may take them to breakfast or lunch and offer a listening ear and demonstrate love. This not only provides a private place for conversation, it also demonstrates a level of concern that in itself will have a great influence.

Team couples should be eager to invest in the lives of their members. Many times we will give large sums to various kinds of Christian work or missionary endeavors, but be reluctant to spend a few dollars at a restaurant as a personal ministry. It has often occurred to me that this level of evangelism and discipleship may have the cheapest price tag of any in existence. We need to use it more.

Use literature . . .

When I know someone has accepted Christ, I immediately send them a note and a booklet, something they can read in ten or fifteen minutes. Or, I may give them two books: one they can read in a brief period of time so they don't get discouraged, and also a longer book.

Not only will the people benefit by receiving the material, but the fact that a leader took the time and effort to write to them quietly communicates how important they and their decision are. How many people do we write to and send books? Not very many. How many notes and books do we get? Not many. Therefore, your note and literature will come across as being very special.

Timing, too, is important. Shortly after people make a commitment to Christ, Satan comes knocking at the door. A leader should write to them immediately so they can have material in their hands at that crucial time. Being a spiritual parent brings responsibility we need to be ready to accept.

Leave them hungry . . .

As the group continues, more and more members will become Christians. A leader should never lose sight of the evangelistic goals, but may want to add thoughts on growth during the group meeting to help some of those who are newly committed to Christ. Even these thoughts on growth can often have an evangelistic application as non-Christians see the potential of the Christian life.

But evangelistic study leaders shouldn't be so growth oriented that they try to make a group into a small home church. People should be left hungry enough to want to be a part of a larger fellowship where there are more opportunities for worship, study and developing their spiritual gifts and service.

Successful avenues for helping people become involved in a church include men's breakfasts, women's luncheons with special speakers, youth ministries, concerts, children's programs, banquets, evening services and film series.

Special events allow new people to come to a church building and meet some of the neat people there without having to make a commitment. They don't come as strangers because they know the person who invited them will introduce them to others. Also, they don't have to attend a worship service which can be very threatening, depending on their religious background. If church programs are geared to the needs of new people, many will want to come back. Many people are looking for the wholesome, positive influence for their families that a church like yours has to offer.

Most of all, pray . . .

The leaders with whom we work constantly remind each other of the importance of the two "P's" — *pray* and *persist.*

We saturate our personal ministry and counseling with prayer. We pray privately and in our monthly leaders' meeting. We pray for the people in our group and for the Lord's wisdom in all we should say and do. We pray and believe God for our group members' spiritual growth and maturity.

Betty is working with several women who, though they came to Christ through one of her studies, have continued to attend their own church where they are not growing at all. She takes them to lunch to encourage them. One is coming with her husband to a new study that just started. Some have been the objects of our prayers and persistence for ten years or more. We won't ever give up.

**For further study —
Acts 20:24-38**

Things I had never heard before

Alf

I came from a typical New England family. One of the things paramount in their minds was to give me an excellent education. I attended Groton, a top notch boarding school and, later, Yale University. As far as any religious belief was concerned, I was an agnostic. My years in college led me to conclude that no one had any answers, so I stopped looking for God. Also, during those years, I could never remember feeling I was getting a good deal from anybody, but always had a negative attitude toward my world.

After graduating from Yale, I went to work for the DuPont Company and had several excellent promotions. Even that did not satisfy me. Moving to Greenville, Delaware, I became involved in the social life there. At the age of thirty-seven, I suddenly realized I was a hopeless alcoholic. What I didn't know was that my wife's contact with a Bible study had started a group of concerned Christians praying for me.

When I began attending a Bible study with Sandy, my wife, I heard *things I had never heard before* — that God loved me, the promise that His plans for me were good. I was impressed by the people who led and hosted the studies and developed confidence in them.

On one occasion, several home Bible studies were gathered into one meeting. There, a prominent sports figure shared how God had changed his life. I knew my life needed changing and could identify with him. My heart pounded with excitement as, at that meeting, I invited Christ into my life.

By far, the most significant blessing in my life has been the fact that my four children have also become Christians. And I find fulfillment in working in a prison ministry and with alcoholics, telling them the same message of God's love I had so desperately needed to hear.

Chapter 11

Gaining Momentum

Betty Jacks

Just as having a leadership team of three couples provides encouragement and accountability, so having several evangelistic Bible study groups within a church, rightly organized and controlled, adds a further dimension of excitement and potential for growth.

There are seasons in a group study. Some studies begin with large numbers and immediate results. Some studies begin with fewer people and require several months of nurture before seeing visible fruit. A study may go through a dormant period or, sometimes, direct attacks from Satan.

A group Dave and Helga hosted seemed fruitless. After the second year they and the other host couple, Don and Ann, felt they wanted to quit. But they prayed and decided to go one more year.

The results were unbelievable. Somewhere between 20-25 people came to Christ that next year. Many of them are now in leadership roles in our church. One woman speaks regularly at Christian women's functions. Another started a Bible study in a local hospital for paraplegics. One of the men is now an elder in our church.

We refuse to allow plateaus to lead to defeat. There are ways to encourage your team, keep their vision fresh and lead them to exciting fruitfulness in ministry.

Bring leaders together . . .

Leadership couples benefit from being together with leaders from other groups. They can learn from one another and receive encouragement. The monthly leaders' prayer meeting provides that opportunity. We call ours a prayer supper. It has been exciting and extremely productive. An effective schedule for that time is:

6:30-7:30 Potluck dinner. While eating, there is a lot of informal sharing about what is happening in the groups.

7:30-8:30 A more formal sharing with reports of progress and problems from each group. A time of sharing solutions and learning from one another, and perhaps developing a strategy for a joint function.

8:30-9:30 Concentrated prayer. If there are two or three groups represented, we often remain together for this prayer time. If there are more than two or three groups, we divide into smaller groups for prayer. We have written lists and pray for every Bible study member by name. One couple we are working with has a prayer list of 70 people.

Combine groups for special events . . .

After forming several Bible studies, occasionally combining them for a special event can add an exciting dimension. It breathes new life into existing groups as members recognize they are part of a larger nucleus of people.

Equally important in a special event is the opportunity for evangelism. Some who have been attending the studies may commit their lives to Christ at the meeting. New people can be invited to attend and they, too, may receive Christ, join an existing study or become the nucleus to form new groups.

To assure success in this special endeavor, leaders should pray for the participants and the people who are being invited.

Present group members should view this as *their* event. If they do, they will respond quickly to the leader's encouragement to bring others to it.

Equally important is that this be a quality event with a good location, good food and an outstanding speaker. The program should be entertaining and fast-moving. Organizers should be sure there is nothing "churchy" about the way the event is conducted. For example, there should be no hymn-singing.

At the end of the program, either the speaker or the host should make clear how people can know Christ personally. One way to get feedback from those attending is to have everyone fill out a card. Organizers can either pass out these cards or have people write on the backs of their name tags. If leaders promoted Bible studies during the evening, they might ask people to indicate their interest in being in a study.

Everyone should be filling out a card, including leaders, Bible study members and guests. This will prevent anyone from being embarrassed.

Some of the questions leaders might want guests to respond to include:

- "What did you think of the meeting?"
- "Would you like to come to more programs like this?"
- "Would you be interested in knowing about a home Bible study to learn more about having a personal relationship with Jesus Christ?"

The host can ask people to place a check mark on the bottom corner of the card if they did pray to commit their lives to Christ during the meeting.

Then, leaders must follow up quickly on those who prayed to receive Christ and get them into a home Bible study.

Special *means* special . . .

A home Bible study operates very nicely in the warm, casual atmosphere of a home with simple refreshments. It succeeds well on the strength of relationships, hospitality, love and straightforward teaching of the Bible.

But if we advertise a meeting as special and encourage group members to bring their friends, we make sure their faithfulness is rewarded. Plan well and provide a good location and program. The results are worth the effort.

An example was a combined luncheon we sponsored for several women's studies. We put a great deal of effort into planning the location, menu and decorations. Our speaker was a famous contemporary artist. Her talk about how she came to know Christ was simple and practical. It was an outstanding meeting. There were about 180 women who came from the studies, including 40-50 visitors.

As a result, there were twelve decisions for Christ and one new study was formed.

Not every combined meeting is conducted on that scale, but the results are well worth making an occasional maximum effort.

Train your members to reproduce . . .

Sometimes God has impressed us with a unique approach to help our group members become involved with us in reaching out to others. For example, on the morning before one of our Bible studies, one of the members of the study asked Bob if he could meet with him for a few minutes after the study that night. He said that he and another member wanted to know more about how they could help their friends and their family become Christians.

As Bob opened the study that evening, he said, "We're going to do something different tonight. We're going to study the Bible for about an hour and then have a coffee break from 9:00 to 9:30. Then, since some of you have asked me how you can help others come to know Christ, I plan to share some thoughts on how you can do that. If any of you would like to stay, we'll begin that session at 9:30."

To our amazement, 17 of the 20 people who were at the study stayed for that later meeting. For an entire hour, Bob had the opportunity to explain and role-play how to be a fisher of men.

Obviously, timing is important. This study had been in existence for two years, so we knew there would be many who would be ready for this step of growth and that we would not cause apprehension by announcing this special session.

As leaders are prayerful and alert, God will show them when and how to involve their members in spiritual multiplication.

For further study —
Acts 4:23-31

Different from anything
I had experienced

Rosalie

I also became a Christian through a home Bible study, but it took two years.

For years I had been searching. I knew there had to be more to life, but I didn't know how to find it. I served on church committees and even taught religion classes, but always came up empty.

When my husband and I were invited to a Bible study, we were happy to go. This was *different from anything I had experienced.* It began to make sense, but still it frightened me because it all seemed too easy. What happened to all those years of work I had done to gain favor with God? Was it all for nothing?

One night, the leader drew a diagram about the return of Jesus Christ on his flip chart. That drawing convinced me of my need to ask Christ into my life. I did, and my whole life began changing from that moment.

Since then, my husband and three boys have all become Christians. Now we, too, are in a home Bible study ministry which averages about 20 people a month, some traveling a distance of more than 20 miles. About 60 different people have come to our study.

Remember me? I'm the girl who took two years to make her decision, but what a joy to see how much has happened since that day. We are privileged to help touch an expanding group of people with the message of Christ.

Chapter 12

Variations

Betty Jacks

The concepts covered in this book are centered primarily around evangelistic home Bible studies for couples. However, they can be used in a variety of ways including:

- Women's Bible studies
- Men's Bible studies
- Youth Bible studies
- Studies in work places
- Campus ministries
- Starting new churches
- Church planting overseas

Keeping standards . . .

I encourage people to think of the home couples' study outlined in the major portion of this book as the norm and to think of other kinds of groups as adaptations. When making a copy from a copy, you lose your standard and quality. You need an original standard against which you measure the validity of other approaches.

There are many opportunities for unique studies — a women's group at a church building, a men's or women's group in an office or work setting, an early breakfast setting, a youth group after school. In many cases leaders will not be able to follow all of the procedures of a couples' study. But a leader should never lose sight of the proven principles behind those procedures. They are a guarantee for effectiveness.

Working with women . . .

With this in mind, let me take you to our church on a Thursday morning. What do you find? An evangelistic home Bible study. A contradiction? So it would seem, but not when you examine what is happening.

It follows the same proven methods outlined for the home studies with four major differences. The study is for women only. It meets at the church building instead of in a home. They meet weekly instead of monthly. They are using a Bible study workbook instead of going through the Gospel of John.

Why did we plan a Bible study with these variations?

One reason is because the study is for women only. There were a large number of women who expressed an interest in a Bible study following the showing of an outstanding Christian film. They signed cards indicating their interest; we called them, and a group was formed.

It's unfortunate when we make our ministry to women an end in itself, capitalizing on their greater availability and interest in the Bible. But it is strategic to take advantage of that opportunity as an avenue to also reach their husbands so their marriages and homes will be united in a love for Christ.

We have seen this happen. Following up these women has often led to a relationship with the husbands, as well. And the women themselves often promote a couples' study in the evening and in a home so their husbands can be involved.

The study meets at the church building because this particular group of women had many children among them and the church building offered the best facilities for us to provide nursery and child care. We hired several women to provide this service, at no cost to the women in the study. Also, women seem to have less resistance to coming to a church building than men do.

The study meets weekly because these women were available for a weekly study. We took advantage of their availability for added impact. In our experience, most men who are non-Christians and outside the church respond far more readily to a monthly study than they do to a weekly study. They resist that heavier involvement.

The women use a Bible study book simply because they will, and this increases learning, as well. In our experience, the non-Christian, unchurched man is more willing to come to a study if he does not have to use a workbook, hold a pencil or even come with a Bible. That's one of the reasons why we furnish Bibles for the group.

Another feature of our women's study is prayer either at the beginning or end of the study. After some months, we have led the women to pray aloud themselves.

When our women's home Bible study ministry had established three or more studies, we organized a coordinating committee. This committee enhances the ministry by getting other women involved in organizing and conducting the special events, inviting more women, helping to keep the content of the studies uniform, and organizing new Bible studies.

Leaders should watch for opportunities to enlist some of the women who attend the studies to become a part of the committee and begin developing them as leaders. They often have great sensitivity to the needs and opportunities in the community. Their webs of relationship often bring in new people for the Bible studies.

Build with strength and proven effectiveness . . .

Of course, we cannot program God and assume there is only one way to have an effective evangelistic Bible study. If a leader pursues these concepts, there may be a time when he or she will use a unique approach.

But we always advise leaders to first use an approach that follows closely the proven guidelines we have presented. This will help assure an initial success, and there is nothing that encourages interest and momentum like success. By assuring that the first groups succeed, leaders prepare the way for a growing evangelistic ministry in their church.

Later, if they try an alternate approach and it does not prove effective, they can go back and evaluate what they are doing in light of the basics, make the necessary adjustments and keep going.

For further study —
Ephesians 5:8-21

I had confidence in the leader

Scott

I was willing to attend a Bible study, but skeptical. The neighbors who invited us were of a different denomination, and I was fearful they might be trying to change my religion.

I knew little about God, nothing about the Bible and had little commitment to the study that first year. We attended on an occasional basis, when nothing better turned up. It wasn't until the Bible study broke for the summer that my wife and I realized how much it meant to us and how much we were looking forward to its starting again in the fall.

With the new start came a change in my attitude. *I had confidence in the leader* and knew I was not going to hear any far-out interpretations.

The third year brought an even deeper commitment. Now we began to work our schedule around the study, making sure that we would not miss a single session.

At the same time, we were experiencing a growing commitment to the church our leader attended. At first, our attendance was very spasmodic, but it grew into regularity.

When, after three years, our leader announced that the study was coming to a close, a feeling of panic came over me. What I had found had become very important to me and I did not want to lose it.

All of these experiences brought me to the place where I finally asked Christ to come into my life. A seed planted several years earlier had germinated and was now bearing fruit. And that fruit is continuing to reproduce, as my wife and I are helping to reach out to others through another home Bible study.

Chapter 13

Making Disciples

Bob and Betty Jacks

A pastor and several lay people canvassed a new subdivision to invite people to come to their church. At one home, a young wife and mother asked, "Tell me, Pastor, where is your church and what do you do?"

The pastor responded by identifying the intersection where the church was located. He went on to list the many services — Sunday School, Sunday morning services and the various mid-week meetings. There were a few more verbal exchanges and the pastor was on his way down the block to another home.

Thinking back on the previous visit, the pastor was arrested in his thoughts. "Where is your church and what do you do?" His answer had been totally inept. The Church is not simply a building on a street corner. Nor is the mark of the Church to hold church meetings.

God's plan for His Church . . .

God's Church is His people, a body formed for the mutual good of all, with varied gifts for effectual ministry in both Christian growth and evangelism.

God's people may inhabit a building, but the building is not the Church. God's people are the Church. In the strictest sense, you cannot *go* to church. You *are* the Church.

God's purpose is ministry, not architecture.

Why is it that he gives us these special abilities to do certain things best? It is that God's people will be equipped to do better work for him, building up the church, the body of Christ, to a position of strength and maturity; until finally we all believe alike about our salvation and about our Savior, God's Son, and all become full-grown in the Lord — yes, to the point of being filled full with Christ (Ephesians 4:12,13).

Seeing our part . . .

The application goes two ways. As members of the body of Christ, we are to function in harmony. We are a chorus, not soloists. We benefit from and contribute to one another. As you serve in the evangelistic home Bible study ministry, your relationship to the other functions of your church body is vital. We all need the edification and encouragement that results from being an active member of a church body.

The verses above from Ephesians also challenge us regarding those who will become Christians through our studies. They, too, have something to contribute to the Church. They, too, have needs that can only be fully met by their becoming functioning members where they can learn from others. They need the opportunities the church provides for worship, learning and service. Plus, these new Christians provide an excitement and boldness the Church continually needs. They also challenge us in new areas of ministry and help keep us relevant.

Beyond evangelism . . .

A leader's ultimate goal for each person in a study should go beyond evangelism to discipleship. In this book we have emphasized keeping the studies neutral, not identified with any particular church or denomination. Their degree of effectiveness depends on that.

At the same time, babies grow. They develop appetites and inquiring minds. This may lead spiritual babies to a vital relationship in a previous church home. Some will not have any affiliation and request information about the leader's church.

What kind of parent are you . . .

This raises questions: Is your church equipped for discipleship? What preparation have you made for additions to your family? Do you have a Christian Education program geared for spiritual growth, not theological debate?

Young parents provide nurseries for their newborn. As their children grow, they adapt to meet their needs at every age level. The spiritually newborn require no less thought and care. They may *survive* in worship services, larger group meetings and adult classes, but they will *thrive* in small groups geared to their needs.

Basic discipleship . . .

A church needs classes geared to newly committed Christians which incorporate these features:

- Small enough to allow everyone to participate.
- A curriculum geared to their special needs and interests: how to pray, how to study the Bible, how to . . .
- Personal and non-threatening to encourage prayer and sharing of needs.

Once a person has completed one or several of the above type classes, there should be the opportunity for a continuing discipling experience. People should be encouraged to be continually involved and not just settle into a spectator's role. Discipling groups should be offered which, in addition to the items mentioned above, also:

- Require commitment from each participant; for discipleship without discipline is not discipleship.
- Offer training and opportunities for sharing Christ's love with others who may not know Him.
- Provide help for people to discover spiritual gifts and find meaningful ways to minister in their church.

The above groups are foundational, but not all-inclusive. God is a God of infinite variety. Workshops, seminars, conferences and retreats can all contribute to building this kind of ministry. Beyond the basics, a church needs a variety of ministries to meet the varied needs of people.

The evangelistic home Bible studies are one way some of your disciples will want to be involved, so these groups will help provide continuing leadership. Other needs and opportunities will emerge as well.

Getting started . . .

Your church or organization may already have many of these discipleship building blocks in place. For you, this evangelistic home Bible study may be one of the varieties of ministry you can add to your program. If so, great! Just follow the guidelines suggested and begin your studies. You'll be glad you did. Greater involvement in reaching others for Christ always adds greater vitality and strength to a ministry. And this will provide another ministry expression for your people.

To us, the important thing is whether you are walking the path of discipleship (as an individual or a church), not how far you have gone. If you haven't started, are you willing to begin now?

Why a "path"? . . .

We think of discipleship as a path, not a sidewalk or a street. A path, because the way is not always easy. There are challenges to face and difficulties to overcome — streams to cross and hills to climb.

But paths also have rewards — adventure, beautiful scenery, reaching out into new territory. May this, too, be your experience in walking as a disciple.

We pray you will find the same joy in reaching others for Christ that we have found.

For further study —
1 Thessalonians 1

The greatest day of my life

*Bill**

I was named "Man of the Year" at my church and was extremely active. For years, I had poured myself into the church and other wholesome community activities. But like so many people today, I went through some very emotional experiences within my own family, including a divorce.

As a result of this and other circumstances, I sold my business and decided to take it easy for awhile. Boredom set in. I decided to seek a management job with another business. I went to work in this small firm and one of the other managers invited me to a home Bible study. I felt I didn't need to know any more about the Bible, but decided to go in order to encourage another man because I felt he needed it.

At the first study I felt a sincere, friendly warmth which I appreciated so much at that time of my life. In the very first Bible study, when I heard the simple claims of Christ, I prayed to receive Him as my Savior. Little did I know what an impact that would have on my life.

Approximately five months later, I was told I had terminal cancer. That was devastating news, but I had a peace which was hard to explain. This news came approximately six years ago, and since that date, I have had 44 different surgeries. The pain I experience is beyond description. I claim that verse where Paul says, "For me to die is gain"; but the Lord continues to use me and I praise Him for that.

I wonder where I would be today if someone had not had the courage to invite me to a home Bible study. I am so grateful. Inviting Christ into my life at that first study was *the greatest day of my life.*

* Since writing this, Bill has entered the presence of his Lord, Whom he met at the Bible study. He is now experiencing the gain that comes through death which he looked forward to.

The Last Word —
You Can Do It

Bob and Betty Jacks

In spite of all our efforts to keep this book as simple, direct and practical as possible, the concept may appear difficult, if not impossible, to many. We can understand that.

In fact, we seriously doubt that a home Bible study of this kind has ever been launched without a great amount of fear and uncertainty. If you are concerned, you are in good company with the many, like those mentioned in this book, who have risen above their anxiety. In leading or hosting a study, they have found joy and fulfillment as others have entered into a relationship with Jesus Christ.

This can be your experience, too. We know you can do it. You probably would not have read this far if you did not have a love for God and a love for those who need to know Him.

Jesus replied, " 'Love the Lord your God with all your heart, soul, and mind.'
This is the first and greatest commandment. The second most important is similar: 'Love your neighbor as much

as you love yourself.' All the other commandments and all the demands of the prophets stem from these two laws and are fulfilled if you obey them. Keep only these and you will find that you are obeying all the others" (Matthew 22:37-40).

There is no greater foundation for ministry. Building on this foundation is not difficult.

To encourage you and help you begin, listed below are some of the practical thoughts we have covered.

Lay people. We, and those with whom we have worked, are lay people, probably much like you are. We are not professionals in ministry, and you don't have to be one, either.

Procrastinating. One of your greatest obstacles is the temptation to delay action. Begin now, while your heart is stirred and your vision is sharp.

Teamwork. Establish a team of a leader couple and two host couples, or, in the case of a men's or women's study, three men or three women. You need the team for support, accountability, the benefit of spiritual gifts and simple manpower to get the job done.

Beginning. Begin with a special event, or by following up an activity at your church, or with a potluck. Use whatever opportunity you have.

Inviting. Invite and invite some more. Never stop inviting, but be content with a small beginning if that occurs. You have read what can result from a small beginning.

Praying. Saturate your study with prayer, but not in the meeting itself. Meet once a month with your co-leaders to pray for people by name and for your communication with them.

Sensitivity. Totally orient your study to relate to the non-Christian. Don't expect the people to adapt to a "churchy" approach or atmosphere.

Follow-through. Be faithful in following through on individuals and needs, even if it costs you.

Expanding. Use special events to add enthusiasm and additional study groups.

Remember, we have known of no failures where the guidelines in this book have been followed.

If you review the above items once again, or even reread this entire book, you can see that none of the thoughts are really profound. Their strength and effectiveness in home Bible studies does not result from their depth.

The power rests in our big God Whose promises and provision we have seen in chapter three. These procedures are simply a packaging of ideas to create an effective environment for us to be the channel of God's power to others.

Yes, what Ken and Rita, Scott and Rosalie and so many others you have met in the pages of this book have done, you can do, too.

I pray that you will begin to understand how incredibly great his power is to help those who believe him. It is that same mighty power that raised Christ from the dead and seated him in the place of honor at God's right hand in heaven (Ephesians 1:19,20).

Appendix

Orientation Seminar Outline

Once you have successfully established your evangelistic home Bible study, you may want to add leaders for more studies and/or share the concept with people from other churches. The following outline can be used to train others informally over coffee or in a large seminar or conference.

The Evangelistic Home Bible Study

To begin this ministry, you may wish to invite people you think would enjoy being leaders and discuss the following:

Objectives

1. Communicate the love of God so others will be drawn to Christ as Savior and Lord.
2. Help new Christians grow spiritually so they can better communicate the love of God to others.

So everywhere we go we talk about Christ to all who will listen, warning them and teaching them as well as we know how. We want to be able to present each one to God, perfect because of what Christ has done for each of them. This is my work, and I can do it only because Christ's mighty energy is at work within me (Colossians 1:28,29).

Resources

1. Bible — God's Word reveals people's needs and the solution, Jesus Christ.
2. Holy Spirit — He brings understanding and conviction to the people in your group, and He empowers you in your role as leader or host.

Dear brothers, even when I first came to you I didn't use lofty words and brilliant ideas to tell you God's message. For I decided that I would speak only of Jesus Christ and his death on the cross. I came to you in weakness — timid and trembling. And my preaching was very plain, not with a lot of oratory and human wisdom, but the Holy Spirit's power was in my words, proving to those who heard them that the message was from God. I did this because I wanted your faith to stand firmly upon God, not on man's great ideas.

Yet when I am among mature Christians I do speak with words of great wisdom, but not the kind that comes from here on earth, and not the kind that appeals to the great men of this world, who are doomed to fall (1 Corinthians 2:1-6).

Then Peter preached a long sermon, telling about Jesus and strongly urging all his listeners to save themselves from the evils of their nation. And those who believed Peter were baptized — about 3,000 in all! (Acts 2:40,41).

But the fact of the matter is that it is best for you that I go away, for if I don't, the Comforter won't come. If I do, he will — for I will send him to you.

And when he has come he will convince the world of its sin, and of the availability of God's goodness, and of deliverance from judgment. The world's sin is unbelief in me; there is righteousness available because I go to the Father and you shall see me no more; there is deliverance from judgment because the prince of this world has already been judged (John 16:7-11).

For when we brought you the Good News, it was not just meaningless chatter to you; no, you listened with great interest. What we told you produced a powerful effect upon you, for the Holy Spirit gave you great and full assurance that what we said was true. And you know how our very lives were further proof to you of the truth of our message. So you became our followers and the Lord's; for you received our message with joy from the Holy Spirit in spite of the trials and sorrows it brought you (1 Thessalonians 1:5,6).

For the Holy Spirit, God's gift, does not want you to be afraid of people, but to be wise and strong, and to love them and enjoy being with them (2 Timothy 1:7).

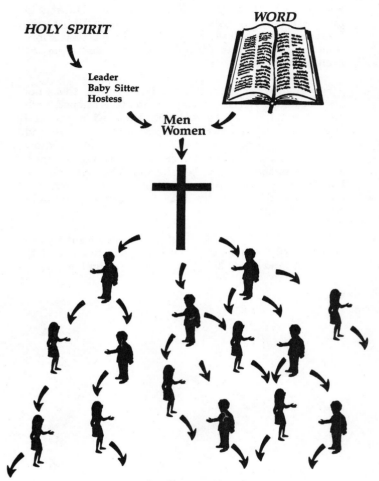

Generations to come

Advantages

1. Built-in contacts

   - Neighbors
   - Friends

- Relatives
- Work associates

2. Non-threatening

- Home setting
- Relaxed
- Non-denominational
- No clergy

3. Leads to follow-up for discipleship

- Over coffee
- Dinner parties
- Social events

4. Prepares reproducers

- They will do it as you do
- They will reproduce others like themselves

How to start

1. Pray, asking God if you should have a Bible study.

- What kind?   Couples', women's, men's, etc.

2. Develop a team.

- 2 couples and a leader
- 2 men and a leader
- 2 women and a leader, and babysitter if needed

3. Set a specific date and location.

   • Second Friday evening in October — my house."

4. Pray, asking God for specific people to ask.

   • Make a list of names.

5. Begin to pray consistently for people on your list.

Invitation

1. Invite

   • Verbally or in writing
   • Don't deceive people; let them know a Bible study is the main event.

2. First meeting

   • Can be a coffee, potluck dinner, lunch, or just a study.

3. Sample invitation:

> Please come to our home for a potluck dinner on Friday, September 30, at 7:00 P.M. After dinner, we will have a discussion on "The Reality of Christianity in Today's World." The discussion will be led by Bob Smith, Field Manager with the Wilson Company.
>
> We do hope that you can come. I'll phone you in a couple of days to confirm and to see what you would like to bring.

4. For lunch or dinner, invite two times the number you can handle.

5. For a Bible study, invite three times the number you want to come.

6. Never worry about the number coming — Christ took time to speak to one person.

7. Expect cancellations from one-half to two hours before the meeting — don't be disappointed.

Elements which will contribute to success

1. Don't invite church friends.

2. Pray regularly.

3. Be lovingly aggressive.

4. Talk about Christ.

5. Be filled with the Holy Spirit.

6. Expect results.

Preparing the study

1. Pray, asking for the mind of Christ.

2. Read through the passage several times, perhaps for your own devotions.

3. Set aside enough time and a quiet place to prepare without rush or interruption.

4. Read through the passage and divide it into easily handled parts.

   ● Paragraphs
   ● Ideas
   ● Several verses

5. Decide on your major objective.

   ● Clear definition of salvation
   ● Instruction for Christian growth
   ● Key thoughts

6. Use several modern versions of the Bible when preparing.

   ● A commentary and dictionary are often helpful.

7. Sometimes what you prepared is not always fully used.

   • Let the Holy Spirit direct.
   • Be flexible.

DO ALL THAT IS HUMANLY POSSIBLE FOR A SUCCESSFUL STUDY. LEAVE THE RESULTS TO GOD.

Leading the study

1. Tell the group our primary objective is to learn more about how God can influence our lives.

2. Introduce the topic of study. Give necessary background information about the Bible passage to be studied or about the book to be used as a text.

3. Tell the group you will read the passage (never go around the room or ask a person to read), and you will not ask anyone to say anything. However, you do welcome questions, thoughts and discussion which will, in the end, make the study more interesting.

4. Hand out a modern translation of the Bible, such as *The Greatest Is Love,* which is the Living Bible from World Home Bible League, 16801 Van Dam Road, South Holland, Illinois 60473.

5. Do

   • Make people comfortable.
   • Provide ash trays. Remember, this is not a prayer meeting. This is evangelism.

- Talk about things people are interested in, before the study.
- Take the phone off the hook or have someone nearby to answer it.
- Include people in conversation. None of your leadership team of three couples should ever be in the same place at the same time, nor should husbands and wives be together. Separate and involve more of your guests in comfortable conversation.
- Be sensitive to timid or turned-off people.
- Provide a copy of a modern translation for each person there, the same copy you use yourself. Then you can direct them to a specific location by referring to page numbers first and then telling them where to look on the page. Many non-Christians would not be able to locate books of the Bible.
- Encourage people to take the Bible home.
- Be sensitive to time. Limit your Bible study to forty-five minutes or one hour maximum.
- Encourage people to ask questions.
- Cover all of the material planned, even if you summarize.
- Have a goal of loving people rather than trying to force theology on them.

6. Don't

- Pray, unless it is a sentence prayer for the refreshments.
- Play religious music.
- Talk about religion or your church.
- Clique with your friends.
- Talk to others in a whisper.
- Berate, or even discuss, religious groups.
- Ask people to read aloud.

- Call on people for their comments.
- Make it "churchy."

7. Questions that stimulate discussion

   - What do you think this passage means?
   - What does this passage tell us about God?
   - What does it say about us?
   - How do you think you could apply the truth of this passage in your life this week?
   - What does this passage mean to you?
   - What do you think God would want you to learn from this passage?
   - Can any of you identify with this person?
   - Have any of you had an experience similar to the one described in this passage?

8. Handling wrong answers to questions

   - Do not embarrass the person by saying flatly, "No, that is not right." If any part of the answer is right, mention that and encourage the one who answered.
   - You may say, "Does anyone else agree with that?" or, "I had not thought of it that way."
   - If possible, try to give another Scripture reference to clarify the answer. Then ask, "What light does this passage throw on the question?"
   - Sometimes restating the question in different words may help to clarify it.
   - Recognize every comment. Call the person by name if you can remember — "Good thought, Bill, but not exactly what I was asking."

9. Handling questions you cannot answer

   - Say, "I don't know!"
   - Ask if anyone in the group has any ideas about the answer.
   - You may suggest that each member of the group should try to find the answer before the next study; if you do, be sure to give an opportunity for people to share what they have found at the next study.
   - Don't argue!!!

10. Be sure every group you lead is centered on Jesus Christ.

    - After preparing a study, think back to see if He is the main emphasis. Remember the objectives of these Bible studies.
    - Stress the good news of the gospel. Avoid negative attitudes and lists of don'ts for the Christian life. Never discuss moral issues.
    - Before closing the study, confront those present with the responsibility to decide for or against Jesus Christ.
    - Use the *Four Spiritual Laws* or other similar tools.

11. Love those you will lead!!!

    - Ask God to love them through you!!!
    - Show your concern and interest in each member of your group. Be available to help if someone comes with a question or a problem.

12. Work out your own clear method of presentation.

- You may observe several leaders for ideas, but *be yourself* when you lead a study.
- At the beginning, get the favorable attention of your group.
- Let them know what to expect.
- Express ideas in as few words as possible.
- Use familiar words — not religious jargon, like "saved," "born again," etc.
- Listen to people.
  - Look at the person talking.
  - Address him or her by name, if possible.

13. Follow up during coffee hour.

- The team should never be together.
- Suggested questions for the team to ask.
  - What do you think of the study?
  - This concept of knowing Christ personally, does that make sense?
  - Have you ever made the wonderful discovery of knowing Christ personally?
  - May I share with you how?

14. Follow up between meetings.

- Phone
- Notes
- Literature
- Personal meetings for breakfast, lunch, dinner

Sample Orientation Seminar Flyer

Learn about a simplified, proven effective approach to

Evangelistic Home Bible Study

(Date)

(Place)

(Time)

This exciting outreach ministry has all these features —

- √ Highly effective in bringing men and women both to Christ and into the church
- √ Adaptable to couples', men's, women's and singles' groups
- √ Utter simplicity
- √ No pressure
- √ Non-threatening to both leaders and participants
- √ Low key

This will be an informal time, giving you the opportunity to evaluate whether you would like to become involved in this kind of outreach.

Each Bible study group is built around three couples, and you can participate in either of two ways:

One couple leads the study of the Bible.
The other two couples serve as host couples to arrange refreshments, do phoning and be involved in planning, prayer and follow-up.

Please confirm your plans to come by phoning:

How to Explain the Gospel

During the course of your evangelistic study, you will have the opportunity to speak individually with people from your group about their relationship to Jesus Christ.

For those who do not know Him personally or are not sure about their relationship to Him, we often use the booklet, "Have You Heard of the Four Spiritual Laws?" (See bibliography.)

The following is another simple way to explain the gospel. Once you learn these four simple steps, you will always be prepared to tell others how God enables us to have a personal relationship with Him. All you'll need is a pen and paper. Another advantage of the following four steps is that, at an appropriate time, they can also be reproduced on a flip chart for a group.

You can use either the booklets or these four steps. If the possibility of knowing God personally is a new concept to you, they will help you establish your relationship to Him. If you already have the assurance of knowing God, they will help you share your faith with others.

"I would like to draw an illustration which shows how God enables man to have a personal relationship with Him.

(STEP ONE — GOD'S LOVE)
"The Bible teaches that God loves man and that He wants us to live life to the full, experiencing such things as God's love, happiness, peace, purpose in life, and fulfillment. Jesus said in *John 10:10*, 'I have come that they may have life, and have it to the full.'

"And not wanting to make us robots, God gave man a will and the freedom of choice.

(STEP TWO — MAN'S PROBLEM)
"But given the choice of either keeping God's commandments (which would lead to a fulfilled life) or disobeying and centering our lives around ourselves, man chose to go his own way. This rebelliousness or even indifference to God is sin. *Romans 3:23* says, 'All have sinned and fall short of the glory of God.' Sin leads to separation from God and eternal spiritual death. *Romans 6:23* says, 'The wages of sin is death.' Man cannot save himself.

(STEP THREE — GOD'S REMEDY)
"But in spite of our sin, God still loves us and desires that we know Him personally. So He Himself paid the ransom for our lives. He sent His Son Jesus Christ to take upon Himself the penalty of our sin, so that we could be forgiven.

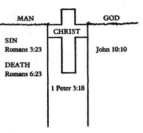

"And since Christ is both fully man and fully God — sinless in Himself and yet bearing our sin — He is the perfect bridge to save us and to restore us to a personal relationship with God. *1 Peter 3:18* says, 'Christ died for sins once for all, the righteous for the unrighteous, to bring you to God.'

(STEP FOUR — MAN'S RESPONSE)
"But while Christ has made it possible for us to cross the bridge to intimate friendship with God, we are not automatically there. We need to take action which demonstrates our faith in what He has done. In prayer, we need to (1) acknowledge to God our sinfulness, (2) ask His forgiveness, which is available because of what Christ has done, and (3) ask Christ to take charge of our lives — to take first place in our thoughts and actions. Jesus says in *John 5:24,* 'Whoever hears my word and believes him who sent me has eternal life and will not be condemned; he has crossed over from death to life.' "

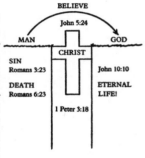

If the person you are sharing this diagram with indicates his readiness to receive Christ as his Savior and Lord, suggest that the two of you pray together a prayer for salvation. Here is an example of such a prayer:

"Dear Lord, I acknowledge that I am a sinner and that I need Your forgiveness. I believe You love me and showed Your love by sending Your Son Jesus Christ to die for my sins. I trust in this alone to put me in a right relationship with You. I ask You to take over my life and live within me forever. Thank you."

Discussion Questions
for the Gospel of John

If you plan to use the Gospel of John in your study, you may appreciate the following discussion questions, most of which have been adapted from *Evangelism for Our Generation* by Jim Petersen.*

In using these questions, we would suggest that you —

1. First review very carefully the content of Chapters 6 and 9, noting especially the suggestions for relating to your group and how to keep participation positive. The importance of that content has been learned and proven in more than 20 years of experience in leading evangelistic studies.
2. Don't substitute these questions for your own personal study and preparation. I spend a minimum of two to four hours preparing for each session and am convinced that there is no substitute for this personal study and prayer.
3. Don't feel that you must use all of these questions. Use only what complements your personal study.
4. Limit the number of cross references you use, as they are confusing to those who do not know their Bible well.
5. Keep the focus on who Jesus Christ is and how we can know Him.

John 1:1-14
1. Why do you think Jesus is called the Word? What is the use of a word among people?
2. Supposing God exists, how do you think a person could come to know Him? What does John say about how one might come to know Him? (1:18).
3. What qualities are attributed to the Word in 1:1-5,14?

*Petersen, Jim. *Evangelism for Our Generation* (Colorado Springs, CO: NavPress, 1985). Questions adapted and used by permission.

4. Another analogy is used to describe Jesus in 1:4-9. What is the function of a light? What are the implications of this title? In what sense are all men illuminated by the Light? (1:4,9).
5. According to 1:11-13, how does a person enter God's family?
6. What do you think John means by "receive Him" in 1:12?

John 1:15-28
7. How would you describe John the Baptist? What did he say about Jesus? How do you think you would have responded to John the Baptist?

John 1:35-51
8. This section relates the stories of five people and the way they came to know Jesus, each one by a different means. Who are they and what led them to want to know more about Him?

John 2:1-11
1. What do you think Jesus' acceptance of the wedding invitation indicates?
2. What problem was brought to Jesus during the celebration? How did He resolve it? If Jesus were who He claimed to be, would this miracle be consistent?

John 2:12-22
3. What led Jesus to act the way He did when He cleared the temple? (2:13-17). How can Jesus' anger be justified? Why didn't anyone fight back?
4. The Jews demanded that Jesus show them His credentials, His authority for doing such things. How did Jesus respond?

John 2:23-25
5. The people believed in Jesus, but He didn't approve of their belief. Why?

John 3:1-15
1. What observations did Nicodemus make about Jesus? (3:1-2).
2. How did Jesus correct Nicodemus? When is someone qualified to understand the things of God? (See 1 Corinthians 2:7-16.)
3. Why does Jesus insist that one must be born all over again before he can belong to God's kingdom? (3:3,5,8).
4. What does Jesus mean by being "born again"?

John 3:16-36
5. The word *believe* appears several times in verses 15-18. What is the relationship between believing and being born again?

6. For what purpose did God send Jesus? (3:16-21).
7. How can one be certain that God is real? (3:31-33 and 7:17).
8. What did you learn about your relationship with God from the study of this chapter?

John 4:1-18

1. The Jews did not normally associate with Samaritans, but how did Jesus show that He accepted this Samaritan woman?
2. How would you describe Jesus' relationship with this woman?
3. Jesus offered "living water" to the Samaritan woman (4:10). What claims did He make about this very special water?
4. What do you think the woman thought Jesus meant by living water? What did Jesus mean?

John 4:19-30

5. Jesus faced the woman with a decision (4:26). What was it?

John 4:31-38

6. What is the harvest? (4:35). Who are the reapers? (4:36-38). Why do you think Jesus is so concerned about the harvest?

John 4:46-54

7. What was wrong with the royal official's faith? 4:46-48). How did Jesus help this royal official come to the kind of faith that truly makes a difference in one's life? (4:50-53).

John 5:1-18

1. How did the lame man demonstrate faith?
2. Imagine being a paralyzed beggar waiting thirty-eight years for an improbable cure. Yet Jesus spoke of "something worse" (5:14). What could it be?
3. What claim did Jesus make about Himself? (5:17-18).

John 5:19-30

4. What kind of relationship did Jesus have with His Father? In what sense was He dependent on Him? 5:19-23).
5. What three promises did Jesus make? (5:24). According to this verse, what must one do to receive these promises?
6. Verse 29 seems to contradict the teaching that spiritual life comes through faith and not through works. How can this be reconciled?

John 5:31-47

7. Jesus stated that there were several witnesses who attested to His deity (5:31-39). Who were they? How did they testify?
8. What obstacle to faith is mentioned in 5:44? Do people still have this sort of problem?

144 YOUR HOME, A LIGHTHOUSE

John 6:1-30
1. What motivated the multitudes to follow Jesus? (6:2,14-15,26-27). Do these same things motivate people to be religious today?
2. How did Jesus react to these people? (6:26-29).

John 6:31-51
3. What was Jesus trying to teach the crowd when He fed them bread? (See also 6:27.)
4. Could Jesus, if He were merely a teacher or philosopher, have given the discourse found in 6:35-38?

John 6:52-65
5. Why didn't Jesus try to smooth things over when He saw that His followers were offended by what He said? (6:60-66).

John 6:66-71
6. Why didn't the twelve leave along with everyone else? (6:68-69).

John 7
1. The primary theme of this chapter is the controversy that continually stirred in first-century Israel over the question, "Who is He?" The people were confused about His identity partly because of their preconceived notions about the Messiah. Do people today have similar misconceptions to deal with before they can come to understand Jesus Christ?
2. How did Christ reveal that He was more than a man?
3. In John 7:37-39, Jesus issued an offer. To whom did He make it? What kind of thirst was He talking about? (4:13-14). Exactly what was He offering? How does one respond to this offer?
4. The guards were impressed with Jesus' words. How did the authorities try to diminish their appreciation?
5. What point was raised by Nicodemus, and how did the authorities react to it? (See 7:51-52.)

John 8:1-11
1. Why did the Pharisees take the woman to Jesus?
2. What was Jesus' attitude toward the woman caught in adultery? Since He did not approve of what she had done, why didn't He condemn her?
3. In what way did Jesus try to confront the Pharisees?

John 8:12-30
4. In 8:12, Jesus said, "I am the light of the world." What does this imply for us?

John 8:31-38

5. Jesus spoke of truth and freedom (8:31-36). What did He mean by "truth"? In what sense do you think truth will free you? In what sense is a person who commits sin a slave to it? What must happen before a person can be really free?

John 8:39-59

6. Why did Jesus say that the Jews who rejected Him weren't sons of God? (John 8:42). How did He prove it? (8:37-47).
7. What are some reasons from this chapter why it is of primary importance to establish a relationship with Jesus Christ?

John 9:1-12

1. What was the disciples' evaluation of the blind man? (9:2). What was Jesus' evaluation of the blind man? (9:3).
2. What happened among the neighbors after the man was cured? Did the ex-blind man's explanation satisfy them? Why not?

John 9:13-34

3. Why was it so hard for others to accept the healing?
4. The neighbors, not satisfied, took the case to the theologians. What conclusion did they arrive at after examining the case theologically?
5. Why did their arguments fail to shake the ex-blind man? Who was in a better position to discuss the subject: the ex-blind man or the theologians?
6. Who finally won the argument? On what grounds?

John 9:35-41

7. How did the blind man become a Christian? (9:35-38).
8. Why weren't these Pharisees able to believe in Christ? Why is there more hope for those who admit blindness than for those who don't?

John 10:1-18

1. This portion gives a parable and its explanation. What do you think is the main point of the parable?
2. What are the characteristics of a poor spiritual leader? (10:12-13).
3. What kind of relationship is there between the sheep and Jesus? (10:14-15).
4. What are some characteristics of the person who follows a faithful leader? (10:3-5,16).

John 10:19-42

5. How is the question, "Who is this Jesus?" answered in the remainder of this chapter?

6. Have you arrived at a personal conclusion on the question raised by the Jews? (10:24). What is the basis for your conclusion? What are the implications for your life in stating this conclusion?

John 11:1-17
1. Observe that Jesus deliberately delayed attending to the urgent request for help from His friends. The result was that Lazarus died before Jesus arrived there. Why did Jesus do this? (11:3-6,11-15).
2. What did Christ want to communicate in the analogy of walking by day and walking by night? (11:9-10).

John 11:18-27
3. What are the implications of Jesus' assertion, "I am the resurrection and the life"? (11:25). What must happen to a person before he can share in this promise? (11:25-26).

John 11:47-57
4. Normally, unbelief is attributed to encountering things that are intellectually unacceptable. But on this occasion, the unbelief appeared in the face of irrefutable evidence. What was the reason for rejecting Christ? (11:47-48).
5. Could these motives still be an obstacle today to people who are considering surrendering to Christ?
6. What was the human rationale used by the high priest Caiaphas to justify the plan to put a good man like Jesus to death? (11:49-50). How did this perspective coincide with God's eternal plan? (11:51-53).

John 12:1-11
1. What did Jesus indicate by His answer that He knew about His near future? (12:7).
John 12:12-19
2. What led the crowd to give this demonstration? (12:17-18).
John 12:20-36
3. According to these verses, what was Jesus' central purpose in life?
4. Jesus said, "The hour has come for the Son of Man to be glorified" (12:23). What was He referring to? (12:27,32). Why was this His glorification?
5. Who is "the prince of this world"? (12:31). What are the implications of this?
6. What lesson was Jesus teaching in His illustration about the grain of wheat? (12:24). How did His death bear much fruit?

7. In the subsequent verses, Jesus extends this principle of death as a prerequisite of fruitfulness to us, as well. How do you think this applies to us?

John 12:37-50

8. Why is it that some people can't believe in Him? (12:39).

John 13:1-20

1. Why didn't Peter want Jesus to wash his feet? (13:7-8). Why did Peter change his mind, asking for a full bath? (13:8-9).
2. What was Jesus trying to teach His men by washing their feet? (13:13-17).
3. Jesus made two assertions (13:13). What are their implications for you? What does He mean by being our "Teacher"? Do you accept Him on this condition? What does He mean by being our "Lord"? Do you accept Him on this condition?

John 13:21-38

4. Why did Judas betray Christ?
5. What command did Jesus give His disciples in John 13:34-35? Why will the person who obeys this command be recognized by all as Jesus' disciple?
6. Do you think Peter was sincere when he made the verbal commitment that he would give his life for Christ? If he was sincere, then why did he fail?

John 14:1-12

1. What do you understand Jesus to mean when He said, "I am the way, the truth, and the life"? (14:6).
2. Jesus tells His disciples they have already seen God the Father. Philip takes exception to this, asking Christ to show them the Father. Jesus responds by reaffirming that they indeed have already seen the Father. In what sense was this true?

John 14:12-20

3. What did Christ say would happen to anyone who believed in Him? (14:12).
4. On what basis could Jesus make such a bold claim to a group of common men who would soon be left on their own? (14:12-14,16-20).
5. Who is this other "Counselor"? (14:16).

John 14:21-31

6. What promise is made to those who, out of love, obey Christ? Why is obedience a necessary requirement to a more intimate understanding of Christ?

7. What does the Holy Spirit do for the Christian? (14:26). How does He teach us?
8. What is the difference between Christ's peace and the peace of the world?

John 15:1-8
1. Vines produce grapes. If Christ is the vine and the Christian is the branch, what fruit does the Christian produce? What are the implications of Jesus' claim that He is the true vine?
2. According to verse 8, what is the purpose of the branch that bears fruit? What does it mean to glorify the Father? What happens to the branch that does not produce fruit? (15:2). What happens to branches that do produce fruit? (15:2).
3. What is the secret of producing fruit?
John 15:9-27
4. According to John 15:9-27, what are some things the person who is dependent on Christ can expect in life?

John 16:1-7
1. In John 16 we see Jesus speaking at length of the provisions He was arranging for His disciples for after His departure. Notice, in verse 7, that He even claimed that they would be better off after He was gone. How could that be true? (See John 14:16-20.)
John 16:8-11
2. What three things does the Holy Spirit communicate to the non-Christian? What does the word "sin" mean in verse 9? According to 16:10, how is justice obtained? According to 16:11, who is under "judgment"?
John 16:12-15
3. What does Jesus promise that the Holy Spirit will do for the Christian? (16:13-15).
4. How will the Spirit guide Christians into all truth? (16:13).
5. What does it mean to glorify Christ? (16:14).
John 16:16-33
6. Jesus foresaw a crisis in the lives of His disciples. What was this crisis? (16:16-22). Why would His departure from them bring about the crisis? What good would come out of this crisis? (16:22-23). Why are crises important for us?
7. It is in this context that Jesus offers us a great spiritual resource. What is it? (16:24).
8. Christ referred to His coming death and resurrection in the expression "in a little while" (16:16). From this chapter, what

are the primary benefits of His great victory over death for the Christian?

John 17:1-5
1. What is your concept of eternal life? What insight do we get about eternal life from 17:3?
2. How can we know God? (17:3).

John 17:4-26
3. What was the work Jesus accomplished for the Father? (17:4).
4. What are some of the works of Jesus described in this chapter?
5. In what way do you wish to participate in this mission? What is your part in this process?

John 18:1-7
1. What steps did the religious authorities have to take in order to arrest and imprison Jesus?

John 18:8-24
2. After stating so boldly that he would never deny Christ, why do you think Peter denied Him three times?
3. What resource do we now have that Peter did not have which can give us boldness and strength as we follow Christ?

John 18:25-37
4. In the civil court, what accusations did the Jews use to obtain a conviction?
5. What conclusion did the civil authorities arrive at after trying the case? (See John 18:38.)
6. The imprisonment and judgment of Jesus underscores the sinfulness of man and the corruption of man's religious and civil systems. What did that time of Jesus' trial reveal about His disciples? (18:8-11,15-18). How can these actions on the part of the disciples be explained?

John 19:1-16
1. What was the real reason that the religious authorities demanded Jesus' death? (19:7).
2. What do you see as the implications of Jesus' statement that Pilate had no power over Him but what was given to him? (19:11).

John 19:17-30
3. What was "completed"? (19:28).
4. Why did God allow all this to take place?
5. The blood of Christ, shed on the Cross, has an important meaning to Christianity. What is it?

John 19:31-42
6. Death on a cross was usually caused by asphyxia (lack of air in the lungs). Thus, in order to make the death faster, the Roman soldiers used to break the victims' legs. No longer able to raise themselves by pushing up with their legs against the cross, thus enabling them to breathe, they soon suffocated. Why didn't the Roman soldiers break Jesus' legs? (19:31-37).

John 20:1-18
1. What were the reactions of the disciples when they discovered that the tomb was empty?
2. What evidences did the disciples have for Jesus' resurrection?
3. What was different about Jesus after He had risen from the dead?

John 20:24-31
4. What is the meaning of Thomas' statement when he recognized the resurrected Christ? (20:28).
5. Normally, what happens when someone arrives at the conviction that Jesus is the Christ? (20:29-31).
6. When He was with the disciples after His resurrection, Christ gave them a mission and the capacity to accomplish it. What was it, and how does this mission affect your life? (20:19-23).

John 21:1-14
1. Peter is perhaps the dominant character in Chapter 21, both by his actions as well as by his conversations. What characteristic qualities of Peter are evident here?
2. What had to happen to Peter to teach him to listen to Jesus?

John 21:15-23
3. What did Jesus want to verify with this series of three questions? (21:15-17).
4. After Jesus verified that Peter was in a position to listen and trust Him, what responsibility did He give to Peter? (21:15-17).
5. Did Peter learn? (See 1 Peter 5:1-14.)
6. One of the first things Jesus said to Peter was, "Follow Me" (Mark 1:16-18). Peter liked the idea, and so he followed. Now, at the end of His earthly ministry, Christ renewed this same invitation! Why was the second invitation more significant than the first? (21:18-22).
7. What results have taken place in your life as a result of studying the Gospel of John?

Bibliography

The following materials are particularly helpful for an evangelistic home Bible study ministry.

Living New Testament

The Greatest Is Love. (South Holland, IL: World Home Bible League).

A paperback Living New Testament which can be purchased inexpensively for distribution, but not for resale. Having a quantity of these New Testaments available at your meeting —

● Eliminates the embarrassment some non-Christians would feel in carrying a Bible or New Testament.
● Makes it possible for you to refer to Scripture passages by page numbers so that everyone can find the passages easily whether or not they know the books of the Bible.
● Simplifies the study by allowing everyone to follow in the same translation.

Resources for Counseling and Following Up New Christians

Ball, Barbara. *Coffee Talk.* (San Bernardino, CA: Churches Alive International).

How to prepare, hostess and speak at friendly evangelistic outreaches. Helpful for planning special events for your home Bible study.

Bright, Bill. *Jesus and the Intellectual.* (San Bernardino, CA: Here's Life Publishers).

A book to help resolve the conflicts that doubters and intellectuals believe arise between themselves and the Scriptures.

Campus Crusade for Christ. *Have You Heard of the Four Spiritual Laws?* (San Bernardino, CA: Here's Life Publishers).

A simple and effective way to tell others how they can know Jesus Christ personally.

Campus Crusade for Christ. *Have You Made the Wonderful Discovery of the Spirit-Filled Life?* (San Bernardino, CA: Here's Life Publishers).

A clear explanation of how to be a Spirit-filled Christian, able to live in moment-by-moment dependence upon God.

Campus Crusade for Christ. *Transferable Concepts.* (San Bernardino, CA: Here's Life Publishers).

Nine practical books that explain the how-to's of consistent, successful Christian living.

Howard, George. *Think It Through.* (Colorado Springs, CO: NavPress).

A follow-up Bible study to firmly establish the new believer in the Christian faith.

Korth, Russ and Wormser, Ron Jr. *Going Up!* (San Bernardino, CA: Churches Alive International).

Leadership concepts for small-group leaders. Includes how to motivate your group, involve them in discussions, encourage participation, vary the format and more.

Lessons on Assurance. (San Bernardino, CA: Churches Alive International).

A Bible study on five key assurances God has promised to all believers.

Lessons on Christian Living. (San Bernardino, CA: Churches Alive International).

A sequel to *Lessons on Assurance* with eight additional chapters on practical areas for growth in the Christian life.

Lewis, C.S. *Mere Christianity.* (New York: Collier Books, Macmillan Publishing Company).

A popular apologetic on Christian belief and behavior to help resolve questions and doubts for those who want to know the truth.

McDowell, Josh. *Evidence that Demands a Verdict.* (San Bernardino, CA: Here's Life Publishers).

A best-selling book on Christian apologetics providing overwhelming evidence for the reliability of the Scriptures, the resurrection of Jesus Christ, and more.

Sanny, Lorne. *Your Decision.* (Colorado Springs, CO: NavPress).

A short, simple study on the Gospel of John, showing the new believer what his decision to receive Christ means.

Stott, John R.W. *Basic Christianity.* (London: Inter-Varsity Press).

An intellectually satisfying presentation of Christian belief and life.

Churches Alive
Helping Your Ministry Succeed

In your hand you have just one part of a wide range of discipling helps, authored and developed by Churches Alive with one overall, church-centered, biblical concept in mind: GROWING BY DISCIPLING!

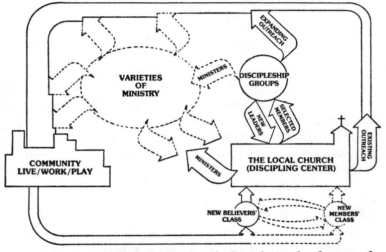

Convinced that the local church is the heart of God's plan for the world, a handful of Christian leaders joined in 1973 to form Churches Alive. They saw a need no one was addressing — someone to work hand-in-hand with the local church to help them develop fruitful discipleship ministries.

Today, the ministry of Churches Alive has grown to include personal consulting assistance to church leaders, a variety of discipleship books and materials and training conferences for clergy and lay people. These methods and materials have proven effective in churches large and small of more than 45 denominations.

From their commitment and experience in church ministry, Churches Alive developed the Growing by Discipling plan to help you:

- Equip people for ministry
- Minister to people at their levels of maturity
- Generate mature leaders
- Perpetuate quality
- Balance growth and outreach

Every part of Growing by Discipling works together in harmony to meet the diverse needs of people — from veteran church members to the newly awakened in Christ. And this discipling approach allows you to integrate present fruitful ministries and create new ones through the new leaders you develop.

This concept follows Christ's disciple-making example by helping you to meet people at their point of need. Then, you help to build their dependence on God so they experience His love and power. And you equip them to reach out to others in a loving, effective and balanced ministry of evangelism and helping hands.

Headquartered in San Bernardino, California, with staff across the United States and in Europe, Churches Alive continues to expand their ministry in North America and overseas.

Churches Alive International
Box 3800
San Bernardino, CA 92413
(714) 886-5361

ORDERING FOR YOURSELF?	ORDERING FOR YOUR CHURCH?

ORDERING FOR YOURSELF?

Your Churches Alive I.D. No.

_____ _____ _____ _____ _____ _____ _____
(from previous packing slip or invoice)

Name _____

Address _____
(Street address required for UPS delivery)

_____

City _____ State ____ Zip _____

Phone (_____) _____

ORDERING FOR YOUR CHURCH?

Your Churches Alive I.D. No.

_____ _____ _____ _____ _____ _____ _____
(from previous packing slip or invoice)

Your Name _____

Church Name _____

Address _____
(Church street address required for UPS delivery)

City _____ State ____ Zip _____

Phone (_____) _____

Pastor's Name _____

Denomination _____

Qty.	Item	Price Ea.	Total
	Your Home, A Lighthouse	5.95	

☐ Please send information about your audio tapes and Discipler's Resource Files.	FREE
☐ Please send information about your consulting ministry.	FREE

Shipping and Handling

All U.S. orders (except Alaska and Hawaii) are shipped via United Parcel Service (UPS), unless otherwise requested. UPS requires a _street_ address.

	Subtotal
Discounts! Subtract 10% on orders over $40.00 Subtract 15% on orders over $100.00!	
Calif. residents add 6% sales tax	
Postage & Handling	
Total	

YOUR AREA	SHIPPED VIA	YOUR COST	DELIVERY TIME
1	UPS	4% of subtotal ($1.50 minimum)	3 days
2	UPS	6% of subtotal ($1.50 minimum)	4-6 days
3	UPS	7% of subtotal ($1.50 minimum)	5-7 days
Alaska & Hawaii	Bookpost	3% of subtotal ($1.50 minimum)	2-4 weeks
Canada	Foreign Book Rate	8% of subtotal ($1.50 minimum)	2-4 weeks

☐ Check No. _____ enclosed made payable to **"Churches Alive!"** Foreign checks may not be accepted unless marked "U.S. dollars."

☐ Please charge my ☐ [VISA] ☐ [MasterCard]

Account No. _____

Exp. Date _____

Signature _____
(required for charge)

In a Hurry?

We can also ship UPS second day and next day air. There is limited UPS service available for Canada. Phone for details, (714) 886-5361.

Mail To: Churches Alive! Box 3800, San Bernardino, CA 92413

Or for faster delivery, call (714) 886-5361

Satisfaction Guaranteed

If, for any reason, you are not fully satisfied with an item you order, send it back in saleable condition within **60 days** with your invoice or packing slip for a refund (less shipping) or replacement. We'll gladly make the adjustment.

Prices subject to change without notice.